MW00990321

THE MANIPULATED MIND
Brainwashing, Conditioning and Indoctrination

Also by the Author

The Whole Mind Book: An A-Z of Everything to do With the Mind (Fontana, 1980)

For Love and Money: The Story of Kim Cotton, Britain's First "Official" Surrogate Mother (Dorling Kindersley, 1985)

Men on Divorce (Piatkus, 1986)

The Hospice Way (Macdonald Optima, 1987)

Cosmetic Surgery (Macdonald Optima, 1989)

The Well Woman's Handbook (Ebury Press, 1995)

Great Ormond Street: Behind the Scenes at the World's Most Famous Children's Hospital (with Alan Sleator) (Ebury Press, 1996)

THE MANIPULATED MIND

Brainwashing, Conditioning and Indoctrination

Denise Winn

MALOR
BOOKS

This is a Malor Book

Published by ISHK

P O Box 381069, Cambridge, MA 02239-1069

First published by Octagon Press, Ltd., 1983
This edition published by Malor Books, 2000

Library of Congress Cataloging in Publication Data

Winn, Denise, 1950-
    The manipulated mind : brainwashing, conditioning, and indoctrination / Denise Winn.
        p. cm.
    Originally published: London : Octagon Press, c1983.
    Includes bibliographical references.
    ISBN 1-883536-22-7 (pbk.)
        1.   Control (Psychology) 2. Social control. 3. Influence (Psychology) 4. Brainwashing.
    5. Behavior modification. 6. Attitude change. I. Title.

BF632.5 .W56 2000
153.8'53--dc21

99-053289

Cover illustration, *Landscape with Figures 1966* by George Tooker
reproduced by courtesy of the artist.

Contents

PREFACE

The Manipulated Mind was written in the very early 1980s. The world is a changed place since then, and yet the findings presented in this book appear to apply just as much today as they did when it was written. Of course, there would have been additions if the book had been written now. There would be more research findings from psychology to enforce the ideas expressed here about influencing feelings, behaviour and attitudes. Questioning of assumptions (see chapter 3) is a large part of what cognitive behavioural therapy is all about – a therapy which really blossomed in the 1990s and which challenges clients to look for evidence for unhelpful beliefs they hold about themselves. The current focus on fostering good parenting skills is a means of challenging old assumptions about childrearing.

Since the book was written, more cults have arisen and more have hit the headlines for disastrous reasons: Jonestown and Waco are two such disasters that leap to mind. More miscarriages of justice have come to light, because of which innocent people have spent years in prisons for crimes they never committed but felt compelled to confess to. The explosion in technology means computer game addicts willingly isolate themselves ever further from normal human contact, and the Internet offers an accessible new medium for advertising and influence. There have been more wars and more crushing examples of man's inhumanity to man.

It all adds up to further evidence for the case made in this book that we are often less self directed than we like to think. I believe the original case still holds good, even approaching two decades later.

Denise Winn
May 1999

1 INTRODUCTION

The term brainwashing made its début in print in an article published by the *Miami News* in September 1950. The author, Edward Hunter, coined the word as a rather down-market translation of the Chinese *hsi-nao*, which meant 'to cleanse the mind', and used the article to claim that post-revolution China was using insidious never-before-known psychological techniques to force the Chinese into the Communist party.

He followed this up with other articles and books on the subject and, by the end of the Korean War, it seemed quite clear to the American public at least that American POWs who had collaborated with the enemy had had no choice. They were the innocent victims of a mind control exercise *extraordinaire*, a technique originally developed to persuade the Chinese of the correctness of the Communist line and then applied to enemy captives.

The 'brainwashing' concept was let loose on a receptive audience. It was a shock, after all, to find that so many of the American boys captured in Korea wavered rather widely from the national line. The exact number of soldiers who, to some degree, went over to the other side, varied according to the sobriety of different source material. Authors, such as psychologist expert Joost Meerloo, who are fearful of the effects of mass manipulation, cite that of 7190 US prisoners held in China, 70 per cent were swayed by Communist propaganda to make confessions or sign petitions calling for the end of the war – though few 'remained' Communist after the war and repatriation. Less dramatic versions of events cite one-third of American POWs taking up the Communist cause. Either way, the figure was high enough to shock Americans into embracing the brainwashing explanation and to numb them perhaps to the equally glaring fact that few British POWs and few, if any, Turks, who suffered the same treatments, capitulated.

The repatriated American POWs became, quite understandably, a phenomenon fit for study by numerous psychiatrists and psychologists, keen to unravel what, if anything, brainwashing was and, if it wasn't, what *had* led their boys to undergo dramatic reductions in their allegiance to President and country. It has been the role of much later investigators of events to posit the idea that the big brainwashing scare was fostered by the CIA.

Hunter, who introduced the term, was, after all, a CIA employee when he wrote on the subject. Not only was he a journalist but a propaganda specialist and had also served as a 'psychological warfare specialist in the Pentagon', according to Scheflin and Opton, authors of *The Mind Manipulators*, who investigated his biographical data. He set the scene in his first book for conveying the message that the United States was under attack by an enemy using secret mind control tactics and that only through equally covert counter-activities could this threat be removed. It is not, however, the subject of this book to look at the resultant activities of the CIA as they 'investigated' the potential of hypnosis, programming, drugs, etc., to gain control of the mind. The several books which have been published on this theme seem to indicate that the CIA reaped embarrassment rather than enlightenment from its efforts.

It is relevant, however, to consider the origins of the word brainwashing because it is an interesting case of a word being coined to encapsulate a concept (for whatever reasons) and then, instead of the concept being the focus of study, the word itself becoming the target of interest. Many psychological experts and intrepid investigators have looked into the subject. Some have concentrated on proving that brains cannot be washed, end of matter. Others have concluded that brainwashing is a powerful, all-pervasive technique allowing first domination of the individual and then domination of the world. Joost Meerloo calls it 'political conditioning' and claims:

> 'Political conditioning should not be confused with training, persuasion, or even indoctrination. It is more than that. It is taming. It is taking possession of both the simplest and the most complicated nervous patterns of man . . . . The totalitarian wants first the required response from the nerve cells, then control of the individual and finally control of the masses.' (From *Mental Seduction and Menticide*.)

And then there is the view, put by Scheflin and Opton, that brainwashing was, and is, an emotional scare word, serving only to prevent our having to face embarrassing or unpalatable truths. It was convenient, for example, to claim that Patty Hearst was brainwashed into taking on the aims of the revolutionary group that kidnapped her in 1974 rather than face the possible fact that even symbols of the success of the American way of life could undergo radical change.

What might now in the eighties seem an academic argument has instead become of new relevant interest, in the light of the recent proliferation of religious cults whose members, many claim, are brainwashed into joining. In March 1981 an English High Court jury decided that the Moonie cult does brainwash people (the word was used), after hearing an action brought by the cult against the *Daily Mail* newspaper which had printed allegations about 'the church that breaks up families'.

The court case has again focused attention on the concept of coercion, unwitting or otherwise, of unsuspecting people. All the old questions have once again been asked. What exactly is brainwashing? Is it possible to force any thinking person to adopt a life-style completely alien to his assumed inclinations? How does brainwashing differ from indoctrination or from the equally insidious influencing effects of advertising or the educational system? Or are they perhaps all the same thing?

Analysis of the concept 'brainwashing' has been made

difficult by the fact that it has never really been accepted as a technical word. The graphic image created by Hunter was perhaps no more than an impressionistic sketch passed down over the years to be embellished or erased according to predilection. For some the picture has very specific component parts, without all of which it could not be seen as a whole; for others it is a blurred canvas and all of human life is hidden there. Such a malleable concept can only arouse fear, contempt or confusion. According to one's definition of the word, one believes in it or one doesn't.

Robert Lifton, who made an intensive study in Hong Kong of a number of Western and Chinese civilians whom the Chinese had tried to convert to Communism after the revolution and published his findings in *Thought Reform and the Psychology of Totalism*, makes a very valuable point in his introduction:

> 'Behind this web of semantic (and more than semantic) confusion lies an image of "brainwashing" as an all-powerful, irresistible, unfathomable and magical method of achieving total control over the human mind. It is of course none of these things and this loose usage makes a rallying point for fear, resentment, urges toward submission, justification for failure, irresponsible accusation and for a wide gamut of emotional extremism. One may justly conclude that the term has a far from precise and questionable usefulness; one may even be tempted to forget about the whole subject . . . .
>
> 'Yet to do so would be to overlook one of the major problems of our era – that of the psychology and ethics of directed attempts at changing human beings. For despite the vicissitudes of brainwashing, the process which gave rise to the name is very much a reality.'

Several psychological experts who examined the American soldiers who were repatriated from Korea concluded that brainwashing was not a new technique but the clever combination of many, each familiar and comprehensible on its own. This present book, aided by the more recent findings about human behaviour that have emanated from the field of psychology, aims to look at those processes which, in sum, have variously been described as brainwashing, to see how each, individually, operates to influence us all in our daily lives. How far do indoctrination, conditioning, need for social approval, emotional dependency and much else prevent us from being as 'self-directed' as we like to imagine?

Demystifying brainwashing, the ultimate change process, can perhaps serve to highlight much about the workings of the ordinary human mind. For the factors that can be combined to force such sudden change are perhaps equally responsible, in their various combinations and unconsciously over time, for the formation of our characters in the first place. It may make us question the foundations instead of the façade.

I am grateful to all the authors of the many books on brainwashing, indoctrination and conditioning that are reviewed in the following pages and should like to recommend the reader to the full bibliography at the back of this book, as all make fascinating reading.

2 BRAINWASHING

To isolate the components of the so-called brainwashing process, it is necessary to take a detailed look at what went on in the Chinese prisoner of war camps in Korea. The American soldiers, repatriated in 1953, who had seemingly collaborated with the enemy and adopted a Communist viewpoint albeit briefly, were not the first to focus world attention on the phenomenon of sudden political conversion. Between 1936 and 1938, Stalin's Moscow Show Trials, where top Bolshevik figures publicly confessed to utterly fantastic crimes that they couldn't possibly have committed – and even seemed to have willingly adopted their prosecutors' view of them as scum – caused alarm to ripple far abroad. That staunch revolutionaries could suddenly have been transformed into grovelling repentants was unthinkable. That some insidious process was at work became a reality for the Americans when their own men later succumbed to the Chinese and made equally fantastic confessions, in some cases, that the Americans had been engaged in biological warfare against the Communists. So the experts were called in to try to find explanations.

Their detailed analyses of the characters of the men, the stresses they were obliged to undergo and the tactics used by the Chinese provide the most comprehensive picture of what has been called brainwashing. In later years, claims made in court that individuals such as Patty Hearst or members of cults had been brainwashed have all been based on the findings arising from Korea.

Different experts have placed differing emphases on the events that occurred and have sometimes offered up differing conclusions. It is worth reviewing their evaluations and drawing together all the common threads.

Edgar Schein, an MIT psychologist, gathered his data in August 1953 at Inchon, Korea, when the repatriates were being processed, and on board the USNS *General Black*, when the men were *en route* back to the United States during the first two weeks of September. In an article called 'The Chinese indoctrination program for prisoners of war: a study of attempted "brainwashing"', published in *Psychiatry* in 1956, he outlined what had happened to the soldiers in Korea, as told by them to him, and drew his own conclusions. He claimed, as a result of his investigations, that there was nothing new and terrifying about Chinese brainwashing techniques. They had, in effect, combined a number of traditional and well-known ploys to weaken resistance, such as group discussion, self-criticism, interrogation, rewards and punishments, forced confessions, exposure to propaganda and information control. What was new was not the method but the manner of combining, in a systematic fashion, a variety of tried and tested methods.

The following description of events experienced in Korean POW camps is drawn from Schein's published version.

The Chinese attitude to their captives differed even at the outset from that of the North Koreans. Whereas the latter were brutal to their prisoners, took their clothing away, deprived them of regular and sufficient food and meted out heavy punishment or death if a prisoner tried to resist them, the Chinese welcomed captives with warmth, even congratulating them for having been 'liberated'.

Over the next weeks and months, however, the soldiers suffered severe physical and psychological pressures and implicit in most of what the Chinese said or did was the suggestion that these stresses would be removed and life be much happier if they took up a more 'cooperative' attitude to their captors.

The men had to undergo long marches, lasting maybe two weeks, *en route* to the prison camp assigned for them. During the march they received little food and, in the interests of survival, were forced to compete with each other for what scant food, clothing and shelter was on offer which, Schein says, made it impossible for them to maintain group ties. Throughout, the Chinese raised the men's hopes by promising improvements in conditions (though stays in temporary camps along the way were no improvement whatsoever) and then dashed them by 'explaining' that the UN was being obstructive or that too many prisoners were being uncooperative and therefore all would have to suffer. Propaganda leaflets were distributed and the men were forced to sing Communist songs.

Permanent camp, when it was finally reached, however, forced the men to suffer physical and psychological stresses far beyond what they had so far endured.

(Schein does not here detail the physical tortures imposed on the men but Meerloo lists a number that were included in official American and British reports. These included:

1. Standing to attention or sitting with legs outstretched in complete silence from 4.30 till 11 pm and constantly being woken during the few hours allowed for sleep.

2. Enduring solitary confinement in boxes $5' \times 3' \times 2'$. One soldier was known to have spent six months in such a box.

3. Having liquids withheld for days 'to help self-reflection'.

4. Being bound with a rope, one end of which was passed over a beam and then around the neck, like a hangman's noose, the other around the ankles. The prisoner was then told that if he slipped or bent his knees, he would be committing suicide.

5. Being forced to kneel on jagged rocks, with arms stretched up above the head, holding a large boulder.

6. Being obliged, in one camp, to hold in the mouth a slim piece of wood or metal that a jailer pushed through a hole in the cell door. Suddenly the jailer would knock the outer end of the wood or metal sideways, usually breaking the prisoner's teeth or splitting open his mouth.

7. Being forced to march barefoot on to a frozen river, where water was poured over their feet. Prisoners then had to

stand for hours, frozen to the ice, reflecting on their 'crimes'.)

According to Schein's account the prisoners had to get up at dawn, exercise for an hour and then, after cereal or potato soup for breakfast at 8 am, spend the day at assigned duties or undergoing indoctrination. Whether a midday meal was served or not depended on the prisoner's 'attitude'.

Living groups comprised ten to fifteen people and the Chinese were careful to separate the men by race and rank so as to undermine the established structure of the group, particularly by removal of leaders. Bearing out the insistence from the Chinese that rank was irrelevant, they were all of one brotherhood now, sometimes very young or bumbling prisoners were put in charge of the rest. If any spontaneous semblance of order arose among the men, the Chinese broke up the group.

Personal affiliations and ties were consistently weakened. The men were not allowed any religious expression and often their mail from home was withheld, though the Chinese maintained that no one was writing because no one at home cared what happened to the men.

Throughout, the Chinese were attempting to recruit men to so-called peace committees. Those that joined then had to play a part in the indoctrination by trying to prevent resistance among the other men and to produce propaganda leaflets to aid the cause, but under the guise of camp recreation activities. Awareness that this was going on made such groups as did form among the men weak and unstable because of fears that informers might be in their midst.

Schein divides the Chinese attack on the Americans' beliefs, attitudes and values into two kinds: direct and indirect.

Direct methods included daily lectures two to three hours in length, the content of which was concerned with disparaging the United Nations, and the United States in particular, and praising Communist countries; forcing prisoners to sign peace petitions and confessions; and making radio appeals and speeches calling for peace. Schein notes that individual confessions regarding the United States' use of germ warfare were particularly damaging to the men who heard them. Whereas most found the lectures naïve and inaccurate, they were more profoundly impressed by explanations of how these bombs had been used by America, put to them by a couple of their own officers who actually travelled from camp to camp for this purpose. Men who had formerly believed the germ warfare accusations to be pure propaganda found themselves questioning their validity after all.

Indirect methods included interrogation on American military techniques which were heavy on psychological pressure. The interrogations might last for whole weeks, with the interrogator actually living with the prisoner and being extremely friendly towards the man. During interrogation, statements made by a prisoner were reviewed repeatedly, in the demand that the prisoner resolve all inconsistencies between early and later versions. When a man refused to answer questions, he might be forced to copy down someone else's answer into a notebook. What might have seemed to the man an ineffectual way of trying to make him change his own opinions to those he was writing was in fact used for a very different purpose: his writings were shown to other prisoners to dupe them into believing that he had voluntarily composed them himself.

All the men were regularly made to 'confess' before each other or to criticise themselves in public if they broke the rules of the camp. (There were very many trivial rules.) Prisoners found this particularly humiliating.

 The Chinese made the most of the effects that the use of rewards can bring. Prisoners who cooperated were offered special favours, food, clothing. Others were tantalised to cooperate by promises of repatriation. The men were also so starved of contact with their families that they would willingly incorporate propaganda peace appeals into their letters home, as they were an insurance that the letters would be sent. Some made propaganda broadcasts purely as a way of letting their relatives know they were alive. Whatever the motive, the effect was that other prisoners suspected they had fully cooperated with the enemy and became mistrustful. So many who lost the friendship of the group continued to cooperate for real.

Schein saw the Chinese tactics as working, in so far as they did, because of the following reasons.

The soldiers first had to contend with immense and debilitating physical privations. In this weakened state, they had to cope with the severe psychological pressure of fear that they would never be repatriated at all or that they would die or suffer terrible reprisals. They were also in a position where their normal beliefs, values and attitudes were consistently being undermined by their captors, thus preventing their maintaining a strong and constant sense of self. The confusion induced could in no way be alleviated by validating themselves against their peers, as group ties were systematically destroyed. Each man was alone to question his role in life. Mutual distrust, fostered by the known existence of informers and the feared existence of informers where perhaps there were none, could only confirm each man in his isolation. The confusion, if it became insupportable, could be alleviated in one sure way: collaboration with the Communists. For that was the only 'certainty' on offer.

The Chinese, for their part, consolidated their gains by other specific psychological tactics. They used repetition to break a man down, making their demands and accusations over and over again until, worn out, prisoners gave in. They operated a careful pacing of demands, starting with trivial requests and gradually working up to the highest demands. They forced the prisoner to participate in his own conversion. Listening quietly to lectures was never enough, the man had to make responses, verbally or in writing. Finally, by couching their indoctrination in the guise of a plea for peace, the Chinese were able to appeal to the all too worn down and war weary soldier.

Schein's view was that no one stress is entirely responsible or overly responsible for the breakdown that can lead to so-called brainwashing. Drs Lawrence Hinkle Jr and Harold

Wolff have asserted, however, that the Chinese made a concerted effort to produce particular emotions in a particular order, which then led to capitulation and collapse. They listed them in an article in the *Bulletin of the New York Academy of Medicine* in September 1957. The emotions to be aroused were: anxiety; suspense; awareness of being avoided; feelings of unfocused guilt; fear and uncertainty; bewilderment; increasing depression; fatigue; despair; great need to talk; utter dependence on anyone who befriends; great need of approval of interrogator; and increased suggestibility. This all culminated in confession, rationalisation of confession and final profound relief.

The US Group for the Advancement of Psychiatry in 1956 held two symposia on forced indoctrination, to which Dr Wolff presented research. He outlined eight of the Communists' methods for achieving the above ends. The description here is based on that in Peter Watson's excellent book, *War on the Mind*.

1. The Chinese enforced trivial demands, such as the keeping of insignificant rules or forced writing, to accustom the prisoners to being compliant.

2. They took pains to show the prisoners that they were in total control of the latter's fate, pretended to take cooperation for granted and tantalised them with possible favours. From this prisoners learned the uselessness of trying to maintain any semblance of control themselves. They learned helplessness.

3. Occasionally the Chinese would offer favours when they could least be predicted, rewarded any show of cooperation, promised better conditions or demonstrated unexpected kindness, all of which served to give the men motivation to comply and to prevent them from adjusting to deprivation.

4. Threats of torture, death, no return home, isolation, interminable interrogation or threats against family and friends served to deepen the men's fears, anxiety and despair.

5. Degradation, such as the prevention of personal hygiene, humiliations, punishments, insults, foul living conditions and no privacy had the effect of making continued resistance

seem pointless and counter-productive. Forced to be concerned only with the most basic of values, it seemed that
compliance could not but help raise self-esteem.

6. By forcing the men to be in darkness or bright light, in
an unstimulating environment without the diversion of
varied food or books or freedom of movement, the Chinese
could force the men to dwell on their captivity, with the
resultant confusion arising from excessive introspection.

7. Complete or semi-physical isolation served the same
ends, as well as depriving the victim of any social support
other than that of his jailer, on whom he became increasingly
dependent.

8. Physical pressures, such as semi-starvation, induced
illness, sleep deprivation, prolonged periods of standing or
interrogation and constant tension, all worked on the men
until they were mentally too weakened to resist.

In an article published in *The Manipulation of Human
Behaviour*, edited by Biderman and Zimmer, Hinkle explained why and how the physical stresses took their
particular mental toll.

The brain's 'internal milieu', he wrote, contains a number
of organic and inorganic substances in solution; disturbances
in the levels of these can adversely affect the way the brain
functions. Not only may the brain itself be directly affected
by these fluctuations but it may also be indirectly affected
when fluctuations impair other vital organs. The kinds of
common conditions which may cause disturbances include
sweating, water deprivation, salt deficiency, excessive water
or salt, vomiting, diarrhoea and burns. Some people when
extremely anxious start breathing too rapidly and this can
cause chemical changes in the blood which in turn can affect
the brain.

Because the brain can only use carbohydrates for energy,
not fat and proteins as can other organs, it is very quickly
affected by any drop in sugar levels in the blood – sometimes
again caused by over-anxiety. A deficiency of B vitamins in
the diet can directly affect the brain. Indirectly, the brain can

be harmed by any malfunction of the lungs, liver and heart, as the efficient working of the brain is dependent on the swift removal of all metabolic end-products present in the fluid surrounding it.

The 'brain syndrome', as it is termed, describes the progressive mental deterioration that occurs when the brain is seriously impaired. Initially a patient is restless and over-talkative, then gradually he becomes delirious, confused and finally loses consciousness. In the early stages, however, there is no obvious sign of brain damage. The patient manifests mainly emotionality, depression, irritability, jumpiness or tension, all of which could be attributed to particular life circumstances. Speech deteriorates slightly and he gets a little vague and forgetful, but the patient can still perform intellectually, if a little less efficiently than usual. Hinkle says:

'In this state the subject may have no frank illusions, hallucinations or delusions but he overvalues small events, misinterprets, blames others and accepts explanations and formulations which he might reject as patently absurd under different circumstances. He does not confabulate but he may be willing to state that a report is "clearly true" or that an event "actually occurred" when in fact the report merely could be true or the event might have occurred. His intellectual functions, his judgement and his insight decline to a similar degree.'

Hinkle suggests that, as the prisoners in Korea were all kept in bad conditions, they might well have suffered these initial stages of the brain syndrome. Also, as the brain needs information of various kinds to process and to keep it active, periods of isolation or the repetitive carrying out of only one mental activity as a work duty were likely to tire the brain and cause it to deteriorate although, again, the effects would not be immediately obvious.

Despite the fact that such physical tolls on the brain must affect its functioning, Hinkle points out that deterioration does not occur at the same rate in all people. He believes that the personality of the individual plays a strong part in determining who holds out longest.

'In short, the brain, the organ that deals with information, also organises its responses on the basis of information previously fed into it. This information, in the form of a personality developed through the experience of a lifetime, as well as immediate attitudes and the awareness of the immediate situation, conditions the way the brain will react to a given situation. There can be no doubt that personality, attitudes and the perceptions of the immediate situation seriously influence the ability of a brain to endure the effects of isolation, fatiguing tasks and loss of sleep.'

Not only does personality affect when brain syndrome starts, it also affects the form that syndrome will take – determining whether a particular man will become talkative, withdrawn, anxious or angry, paranoid or trusting.

He ends by saying, 'Disordered brain function is indeed easily produced in any man. No amount of "will power" can prevent its occurrence.'

Psychologist Joost Meerloo draws on psychoanalytic and conditioning theory to explain the brainwashing of the American soldiers. He coined the term 'menticide' to describe it. Meerloo was a one-time chief of the Netherlands Forces psychology department who became an American citizen in 1950. He was called as an expert to give evidence to the military inquiry on the Colonel Schwable case. (Colonel Schwable, an officer of the US Marine Corps, 'confessed' in Korea that America had been carrying on bacteriological warfare against the enemy, citing supposed missions, meetings and strategy conferences as well as naming names.)

Meerloo's position is that successful menticide techniques make full use of people's deep underlying guilt feelings and their unconscious need to be conditioned by and conform to traditional patterns. He believes people fear the freedom and the conflicts that complete autonomy brings.

He actually claimed that the Chinese capitalised on the findings of Russian physiologist Ivan Pavlov in regard to conditioned behaviour. Pavlov discovered that he could make dogs salivate when they heard a bell. By ringing a bell whenever he gave them food, he led them to associate the two events. He had 'conditioned' an unnatural response. He went on from this discovery to find out much about conditioned behaviour (see Chapter 4) and the circumstances that could facilitate or impede it.

One such finding that Meerloo believes the Communists picked up was the fact that conditioning could most easily be effected if the process was carried out in a quiet environment with few distracting stimuli. Political victims, therefore, were more easily conditioned if kept in isolation from each other.

It was Pavlov who first found that some animals learn more quickly if they are rewarded for doing so, by affection or the giving of food, whereas others responded more effectively if they suffered a painful penalty for mistakes. The differences, Meerloo suggests, are likely to be related to the nature of earlier conditioning by parents. As, in people, the effect might be that one person could resist indefinitely in the face of punishment whereas he could easily be won over by rewards, interrogators could not use rewards and punishments indiscriminately if they wanted results. They knew that they had to find out first which category their prisoner belonged to.

The use by the Chinese of boring repetitive routines was based, says Meerloo, on the Pavlovian finding that any kind of previous conditioning, no matter how strong, could be rendered ineffective – inhibited – by boredom.

Finally, he suggests that the Chinese developed a suggestion made by Pavlov that weak, secondary stimuli could also have conditioning qualities – the tone in which words are spoken being as effective as the actual words used for shaping behaviour. Pavlov didn't pursue this area of thought far but, in the 1950s, the role of linguistics in mass indoctrination was studied by other Russian physiologists.

Meerloo is careful to state, however, that it is too simplistic to believe that permanent changes can be made to a person's thoughts and behaviour just by straightforward application of Pavlovian theories of conditioning. He does believe that it can be a powerful means for capitalising on the deeper emotional insecurities of man, once aroused. For instance, in isolation, when a prisoner is closed off from the world and deprived of the usual range of stimuli from the senses, his mental activity changes. He starts to dwell on long forgotten anxieties that rise to the surface and his fantasy life grows more real than his real life. In that state he is vulnerable, as he cannot check the validity of his feelings and fantasies against ordinary reality.

In fact, far from saying that conditioning of behaviour is the main thrust of brainwashing techniques, Meerloo emphasises that a human being's own basic drives and needs can lead him unwittingly to take a part in the brainwashing process. Need for companionship doesn't disappear when a guard or an interrogator is the only person available who could possibly offer it. Few personalities, he says, can resist the need to yield if they are suffering overwhelming loneliness. The first step towards yielding may well be that the prisoner, when in isolation and convinced, by the enemy, that everyone has deserted him, accepts and even welcomes the jailer as a substitute friend.

Similarly, the victim may have to 'pay' for his capitulation, his (to himself) unforgiveable need to draw comfort and friendship from whatever source he can, by becoming even more cruel to himself than the inquisitor could be. This passive attempt at annihilating the enemy adds even more stress to an already intolerable load: the prisoner is fighting himself as well as his captors, leaving himself doubly weakened.

Just as successful brainwashing cannot be achieved by the cold application of techniques that take no account of the prisoner's personality, his fear, insecurities and basic needs, so, says Meerloo, training soldiers to withstand physical tortures is for similar reasons ineffective as a method to help them resist being brainwashed by captors. It is not physical torture that is the most effective weapon of brainwashing;

the very teaching of evasive techniques to withstand torture can itself induce psychological reactions in the soldiers so trained that can work against their resistance, not for it. The aroused anxiety and the dread anticipation, knowing what may happen, can lead a prisoner to capitulate all the sooner. It is only by applying effective mental strategies that anyone can resist and those mental strategies have to be drawn from a balanced perspective on life. Without that perspective operating in ordinary daily life, they cannot be pulled out of the hat ready to apply when or if one suddenly finds oneself in a powerful coercive and unnatural milieu. (See Meerloo's *Mental Seduction and Menticide.*)

Robert Lifton's study of brainwashing techniques (which he termed thought reform) also relies for its conclusions on psychoanalytic theory. Lifton took part in the examination of the American POWs on the troopship back to the United States but his real work began when he went to Hong Kong and interviewed in depth a number of Western and Chinese civilians who had been living in China at the time of the Communist takeover in 1948. Subsequently they had escaped to Hong Kong. In his book *Thought Reform and the Psychology of Totalism*, he described and assessed the experience of fifteen Chinese intellectuals who had undergone reform in universities and revolutionary colleges and twenty-five Westerners who were believed by the Chinese to be antagonistic to the Communist régime and underwent reform in prisons.

One of the Westerners was a Frenchman, Dr Charles Vincent, who had lived and worked in China for twenty years before his arrest. Accused of being a spy, he was in prison for three and a half years. Of him and another prisoner, Father Luca, both of whom were trapped into making extensive confessions of acts never carried out, as well as unfounded denunciations of friends, Lifton said:

'. . . Their environment did not permit any side-stepping: they were forced to participate, drawn into the forces around them until they themselves began to feel the need to confess and reform. This penetration by the psychological forces of the environment into the inner emotions of the individual person is perhaps the outstanding psychological fact of thought reform.'

Lifton identified the processes at work as follows:

1. *Assault on identity* Dr Vincent was told that he was not a real doctor, Father Luca that he was not a genuine Father. Both as they began to lose their bearings started to question what and who they were.

2. *Guilt* Both men found themselves condemned by an infallible environment. They became so permeated by an atmosphere of guilt that the accusations being levelled at them merged with subjective feelings of sinfulness and having done wrong. They knew they were guilty of something, they felt very guilty, and gradually grew to believe that punishment must be deserved.

3. *Self-betrayal* The denunciation they were forced to make, of friends and colleagues, had a dual effect. It increased their feelings of guilt and shame. But, equally fundamental, by denouncing all those with whom they had associated in their lives, they were effectively denouncing all that their lives had been up till that point. They were not so much betraying friends as being forced to betray the vital core of themselves.

4. *Breaking point* The combined effects of severe guilt, shame, and self-betrayal led them to feel alienated from themselves. They began to fear total annihilation and as everything that happened fanned rather than dispelled that fear, they moved inexorably towards breakdown.

5. *Leniency* The inevitability of total annihilation would suddenly be overturned by a showing of unexpected leniency on the part of their captors. A brief rest from interrogation, a brief encounter in which they were treated momentarily as individuals, summoned for the men a spark of renewed identity. Suddenly, annihilation was not the only outcome they could envisage. Annihilation could – and now

must – be avoided and there was only one immediate way to achieve that. For a man in such a position, said Lifton, 'the psychological decompression of his environment serves to win him over to the reform camp'. The men virtually became grateful participants in their own reform.

6. *The compulsion to confess* Confession, in that it offered a way to resolve the overwhelming guilt engendered, gradually became more and more attractive. The compulsion to end the horrors of confusion and identity loss by owning up to that guilt was finally irresistible.

7. *The channelling of guilt* The amorphous, formless guilt that had been drawn from within them could be given an understandable form if they adopted the 'people's standpoint'. Their guilt could be attributed to a life of wrong action created by a wrong ideology.

8. *Re-education: logical dishonouring* To achieve 'true' re-education, the prisoners had to extend their self condemnation to every aspect of their former lives – to see their lives as a long series of utterly shameful acts.

9. *Progress and harmony* The rightness of their new, reformed position was reinforced by the many emotional needs that were met as a result of their holding it: they could feel group intimacy in their living and working, they could participate in pursuing a common goal, they could experience the relief of solving all problems, resolving all confusion. Instead of alienation, they could experience themselves as in harmony with their surroundings.

10. *Final confession and rebirth* In this new spirit of harmony, the men were fully ready to supply with conviction statements about what they now were and what they had rejected. They experienced a virtual rebirth.

Lifton claimed that, in all the cases of apparent conversion, similar emotional factors seemed to be played on: particularly, a strong and readily accessible negative identity, an unusually strong susceptibility to guilt, a tendency towards identity confusion (particularly if a cultural outsider) and an all-or-nothing type of emotional set.

Particularly interesting, however, was Lifton's finding that those who appeared to resist reform during their prison experience had similar characteristics. They also had the tendency towards needing to go wholeheartedly one way or the other and, by their habitual use of denial and repression to keep themselves in check, ended up in the situation where those least threatened by the power of the brainwashing techniques actually feared they were in most danger of capitulating to them. Although they were seemingly resisters, they were in a constant struggle against the desire to capitulate.

Lifton pinpointed the features which seemed to him to be characteristic of ideological totalism and necessary for the maintenance of its hold over individuals: control over all forms of communication; mystical manipulation (totalism as a furtherance of established higher purposes); demands for purity; creation of a cult of confession; stress on 'sacred sciences'; loading of language (what Lifton calls thought-terminating clichés); putting doctrine above the person; and the 'dispensing of existence' – deciding those who have a right to exist and those who don't.

Schein, Hinkle, Wolff, Meerloo and Lifton all agree that personality was an important factor in whether an individual capitulated to or resisted Communist influence. All have said, in one form or another, that those with well-integrated, stable personalities were the ones least susceptible to psychological pressure. However, Dr William Sargant, a British psychiatrist, believes that what happened in Korea was just one form of the sudden conversion syndrome, a phenomenon which can be explained by physiology alone. Personality, in so far as it plays a part in Sargant's thinking, dictates not ability to resist but length of time it takes to collapse. People of stable personality may take longer to fall, he says, but far from being immune, they are the most likely to remain faithful longest to their newly implanted convictions. (He believes that had it not been for language difficulty and a certain unsubtlety of technique, the Chinese could certainly have won over more soldiers.)

Sargant offers a package to explain what he sees as the inevitability of conversion once the right stresses are imposed on the brain. He explains dramatic religious conversion, brainwashing or dramatic political conversion, false confessions and psychoanalytically-induced insights by physiological events to which only certain mentally ill people are immune. He relies for his assertions on the work of Pavlov. Unlike Meerloo, he doesn't claim that the Chinese achieved what they achieved because they studied Pavlov but he does believe that Pavlov's findings regarding reactions to stress are the key to understanding any sudden conversion, political or religious. He says, in *Battle for the Mind*, where he explains his theory, 'The politico-religious struggle for the mind of man may well be won by whoever becomes most conversant with the normal and abnormal functions of the brain and is readiest to make use of the knowledge gained.'

Sargant's interest in the work of Pavlov stemmed from his experiences during the Second World War, treating shell-shocked soldiers. His reading of Pavlov threw light, for him, on why the soldiers recovered from mental breakdown if they could be induced to experience emotional discharge of an intense nature, and led him to posit that the success of religious and political conversions was based on the manipulation of the same physiological processes.

In the course of his work on conditioned learning in dogs (see Chapter 4 for a full explanation of conditioning), Pavlov started to make discoveries about the dogs' reactions to stress. He found that his dogs could be divided into four temperament types. The first two he called 'strong excitatory' and 'lively', the second group being less extreme in their excitability, but both groups likely to respond to stress by showing heightened excitement and aggression. The other two types were more passive in their reaction. One Pavlov termed the 'calm imperturbable' type, the other the 'weak inhibitory' type. This last group tended to react to stress with extreme passivity in order to avoid tension. Strong experimental stresses reduced such dogs to a state of paralysis and an inhibition (or blocking) of brain function. However,

Pavlov found, the other three types of dogs, if exposed to more stress than they too could stand (the amounts being higher than for the weak inhibitory type), also reached a state of brain inhibition. He decided that this inhibition must therefore be a protective mechanism designed to protect the brain when the system was pressed beyond all endurance. Which category a dog fell into was decided, he believed, by environmental stresses to which it had been exposed right from birth and to which it had been conditioned to react in particular ways, in accordance with its own temperament. Lively and calm, imperturbable dogs could withstand much more stress than either strong or weak excitatory types.

The inhibition which occurred when all dogs had passed their limit of endurance (Pavlov called it transmarginal inhibition) had definite stages of build-up, signalled by particular abnormal behaviour patterns. Pavlov found that he could induce brain inhibition by imposing four different types of stress and monitor the development of the abnormal behaviour.

To induce the intolerable stress, he would increase the voltage of electric shock applied to the dog's leg as part of its conditioning process. If the shock was too strong for its system to tolerate, the dog started to break down. Another method was to signal the arrival of the dogs' food and then make them wait a long time for it to appear. The dogs reacted very quickly to waiting under stress. Thirdly, he might confuse the dogs by giving them conflicting signals, so that the dogs became uncertain what to expect. Finally, he might induce stress by physical means, such as overworking them or depriving them of food.

Pavlov found that if he first wore down the dogs in one or more of these ways, new conditioned behaviour patterns – such as responding to a given signal in a given way – were much easier to implant. However, whereas the weak inhibitory type dogs broke down much faster, they were likely to forget those new behaviour patterns once they recovered. The dogs that were harder to break down were more likely to hold on to the behaviour patterns for a long time after.

Pavlov presumed that, due to temperament, they held on to the new patterns as tenaciously as they had once held on to their old ones.

During this whole process, Pavlov isolated three distinct stages that led on to collapse as extreme stresses mounted. First came what he termed the 'equivalent' phase of brain activity, when a dog would react in the same way to all stimuli of whatever strength. (Pavlov measured this by saliva production.) One might equate this with the familiar phenomenon of a person reacting no more strongly to an important experience than to a trivial one: the exhausted woman who receives a cup of tea and the news that she has won the football pools with equal mild pleasure.

When exposed to even stronger sustained pressures, the dog would move into what Pavlov called the 'paradoxical' phase. Here, the brain would cease to react to strong stimuli at all, as a protective measure, while still capable of responding to mild ones. This therefore gave rise to a circumstance which, in humans, could be manifested as an inability to cry on hearing of the death of a loved one but to be intensely irritated and upset by the loss of an ear-ring.

The third and final stage of brain inhibition Pavlov called 'ultra paradoxical'. Now the dog reacted with a positive response where normally it had a negative one and vice versa. For instance, it would try to elicit affectionate attention from a laboratory assistant it had previously disliked, and attack one it had previously been fond of.

Once these three stages had been set in train, Pavlov noticed, the dogs often behaved in a hypnoidal fashion. Sargant remarks that clinical reports of patients under hypnosis often reveal them to act in ways consistent with Pavlov's inhibition phases.

A final unexpected discovery occurred for Pavlov when his dogs were nearly drowned during the Leningrad floods, as they were trapped in their cages. At the last minute a laboratory assistant was able to rush in and save them but the terror of the experience, a stress beyond all stresses, produced yet another brain response. The dogs forgot all that they had been taught by conditioning up to that point. That is, all the conditioned reflexes that Pavlov had implanted in them had vanished and it took months to restore them.

Pavlov believed that the higher centres of the brain in dogs and in humans were in a constant state of flux between excitation and inhibition; that when one part was highly excited, another area was inhibited as a result. For instance, a person undergoing an ecstatic experience may be temporarily oblivious to pain. He also noted that one part of the brain cortex which had been over-excited might become fixed, leading to a pattern of repetitive movements or behaviour. He thought this might explain, for example, obsessional thinking.

Sargant uses these findings from Pavlov to extrapolate about the mechanisms of recovery from shell-shock, religious conversions, and the eliciting of false confessions. (He maintains that those who believe the exercise of will-power is sufficient to beat the brainwashers are sadly mistaken. Active resistance only puts yet more pressure on the brain and speeds breakdown.)

After his reading of Pavlov's work, Sargant says he became aware how far the behaviour of shell-shocked soldiers whom he was treating at the time accorded with Pavlov's inhibition stages. Some, for instance, might be suffering severe fright paralysis of the limbs. If they tried to move them, they couldn't. But if they were thinking about something else, they were amazed to find that they *could* move the paralysed limb – an example of the paradoxical stage, says Sargant.

Men who came to the clinic in a state of nervous breakdown and emotional paralysis could be released from their suffering if Sargant induced an abreaction – an intense emotional discharge. This might be achieved by giving them a drug to help lower their defences and then coaxing them to talk of the experience they had had and which they had, till now, repressed. If the soldiers could be drawn to the limits of their endurance in this way, they experienced a sudden intense outpouring of their feelings and a reliving of the events in question, an exhausting experience that led them finally into emotional collapse. When they came out of it, they were like different men. They could see what had happened in perspective, they could face up to the horrrors and fears they had undergone in the trenches.

The principle of emotional discharge, the release of locked-in emotions, is behind most modern psychotherapies. However, Sargant makes a significant point. The abreaction could be induced even if the events being reacted to were implanted by the doctor and had never happened. For instance, the doctor might ask the patient to describe himself fighting his way out of a burning tank and the patient would eventually experience emotional collapse, even though the event had never happened. What is vital, to Sargant, therefore, is not the unblocking of repressed memories and their concomitant emotions but the build-up of stress to its extremes, by whatever means, with a view to eliciting a freeing emotional discharge.

After the abreaction was over, the men lost their fright paralysis or whatever compulsive behaviour pattern had been established. All that neurotic behaviour had been knocked out by the collapse. Sargant sees this as akin to what happened with Pavlov's dogs.

In using Pavlov's findings to explain seemingly inexplicable religious and political conversions, Sargant stresses the suggestibility state that is engendered as a result of extreme anxiety. He recalls how the terrors of the Blitz enabled large numbers of people to believe unlikely stories, such as the rumours following Lord Haw-Haw's broadcasts from Germany. Sargant relates such occurrences back to Pavlov's finding that, once extreme stress was induced, dogs could be made to give up their old conditioning in order to take on the new set of responses conditioned by the laboratory assistants. And, if they were of balanced temperament, they would hold on to those new behaviour patterns as firmly as they had resisted losing the old.

Sargant sees this mechanism working in revivalist meetings, where extreme emotional stress induced by the preaching, the atmosphere, the guilt and fear, led to collapse and then adoption of the new thinking. Similarly, in Korea, the Chinese in effect used the same breakdown system to implant a new set of beliefs. Pure intellectual indoctrination, he says, would be useless.

A proof that it is stress of any kind that is the key to conversion, rather than underlying sympathy with the new views, might be, as Sargant suggests, the fact that those who attended Wesley's evangelistic meetings and were roused to a pitch of anger and indignation at what was going on were just as likely to break down under the stress of the negative emotion – and come to, saved. Sargant also cites Arthur Koestler's account of the night he made his decision to become a Communist (he remained with the party six years). Koestler himself says that a whole series of 'grotesque events' clinched the making of a decision he had been moving towards for some time. The events in question were a heavy hangover, a broken down car, a heavy financial loss at poker and a drunken sexual encounter with a person he disliked. None of the stresses were connected with or threw light on his position as regards Communism but they precipitated his sudden decision to join the party.

Any extreme experience of emotion can make a person highly suggestible and either reverse his conditioned behaviour patterns or else wipe them out altogether, according to Sargant. The degree of stress and the individual's level of ability to withstand stress will determine the actual outcome.

Sargant does not claim that every single person can be brainwashed. He excludes certain categories of the mentally ill whose emotions are so impossible to arouse or who are so disconnected from their feelings that they cannot be brought to collapse. Such people cannot be made to abreact in hospitals, for instance.

However, he does say, in connection with brainwashing: 'Granted that the right pressure is applied in the right way and for long enough, ordinary prisoners have little chance of staving off collapse; only the exceptional or mentally ill person is likely to resist over very long periods. Ordinary people . . . are the way they are simply because they are sensitive to and influenced by what is going on around them; it is the lunatic who can be so impervious to suggestion.'

Psychological factors in the brainwashing process are not ignored by Sargant. He considers the guilt, isolation, physical weakening, etc., are all a vital part of the build up to intolerance level. But the conversion experience itself he sees as due to the physiological events happening in the brain, an inevitability of our physical make up. He therefore offers different explanations for actions which others see as based in our emotional drives and needs as human personalities.

He suggests, for instance, that 'one of the more horrible consequences' of interrogations where the victims suddenly start to feel great affection for an interrogator who has been treating them ruthlessly, is a warning sign that the ultra-paradoxical stage of abnormal brain activity may have been reached. The victim likes instead of hates his persecutor. Others, already mentioned, tend to put such seemingly contradictory behaviour down to the fact that human beings need warmth and attention from at least someone and if the interrogator is the only one around to provide it, then his will have to do. Ian McKenzie, writing on hostage-captor relationships in the *Bulletin of the British Psychological Society*, thinks that Aronson's gain-loss theory may also have some bearing: the theory suggests that increases in positive, rewarding behaviour from another person have more impact on someone than consistent, unvarying ap-proval. Respect or liking has to be won, it can't be taken for granted. Therefore, when it is given in any little way, it means more, or has more immediate effect, than liking that exists regardless.

Sargant has been much attacked from many quarters for his firm adherence to a physiological explanation for brain-washing and sudden conversion and the kind of examples of behaviour that he uses to support it.

Psychologist T. H. Pear, in *The Moulding of Modern Man* makes a lyrical objection. He doesn't mention Sargant by name but his approach is clearly covered by the criticism and *Battle for the Mind* is listed in the Bibliography. Pears said:

'The inventor of the term "brainwashing" deserves no thanks from anyone trying to understand the techniques, some ham-handed, some astute but sporadic and others cleverly integrated, which are given that name. The word, misleadingly descriptive, attracts those who believe that the only way to unravel the mind's workings is to grasp the activities of the brain; presumably, to explain the physical events occurring when a gramophone record is played may lay bare the whole story of Verdi's *Requiem*, including his temperament and the religion which inspired him, not to mention the mental processes of the singers and the conductor.'

Dr James A. C. Brown, a British psychiatrist who died in 1964, also thought that Sargant was rather short on acknowledgement that there is a man behind the brain cells.

His own starting point, in his *Techniques of Persuasion*, is the belief that people's attitudes in life are not all of the same strength and permanency, by their very nature. Only some attitudes can be changed by other people, others never. The deep attitudes are those which develop from an early age and create a perspective on life which rarely alters; the less entrenched attitudes are those that might more correctly be called opinions and which are much more amenable to alteration. Furthermore, what may seem to be radical changes in a person's beliefs are in fact most likely in keeping with their basic character anyway. Brown says:

'Opinions are but briefly held and likely to reflect current public feeling; in many cases they reflect rather what the individual thinks he should feel than what, in fact, he does feel. They are readily changed and may be susceptible either to propaganda or to reasoned argument. Attitudes, on the other hand, are likely to be long-lived and do not necessarily reflect the feelings of the general public although they tend to reflect those of some group with which the individual has become associated. Ordinarily they are rooted in character traits which cause the individual to select from the flood of stimuli constantly impinging upon his senses only those which are consonant with his own deep-rooted beliefs. Although they are capable of changes which are quite real in the social sense, these changes are apt to be more apparent than profound. Thus the change from Communism to Fascism or, in the field of religion, to Roman Catholicism, is quite real socially in that these bodies proclaim vastly different doctrines which result in entirely divergent behaviour, but emotionally and from the standpoint of character all are on the same level on the authoritarian-democratic scale because all share the same attitude toward authority.'

Therefore, when he talks specifically about brainwashing he says, 'Despite their great doctrinal differences, all forms of totalism are brothers under the skin and appeal to the same type of person and those "converted" by brainwashing in any final sense are converted not in spite of, but because of, themselves.'

Brown, while acknowledging the value of Pavlov's findings about stress behaviour, rejects the interpretation put on them by those keen to show that brainwashing techniques can literally reverse human behaviour. He finds even Pavlov's assertions suspect in this area: for instance, is it such an inexplicable and sudden reversal of behaviour for a dog which liked a laboratory assistant and then gets tormented by him in experiments to turn against him afterwards? Similarly he finds suspect cases cited by Pavlovian disciples to prove the 'same' things happen in humans: a woman who suddenly wants to kill the child she loves doesn't manifest such feelings out of the blue; they were there in some form all along and were kept repressed until they overflowed into consciousness, he says.

The Reverend Ian Ramage is upset by what he sees as Sargant's somewhat over-generous application of Pavlovian findings to events in the ordinary world. He finds large structural flaws in Sargant's reasoning – particularly as regards Sargant's claim that the religious conversion syndrome is all due to goings-on in the brain cortex. Of course it is his particular interest to disprove such a connection but his reasoning is clear and worth consideration: in his *Battle for the Free Mind* he makes a distinction between breakdown and emotional abreaction, whereas Sargant appears to link them:

'In the traumatic experiences which lead to battle neurosis and the terrors deliberately imposed in brainwashing, we may well have processes roughly parallel to the experimental stress situations imposed on Pavlov's dogs, resulting in various stages of abnormal behaviour and culminating in terminal exhaustion and collapse. However, it must be pointed out that nowhere in these experiments with dogs, as described either by Dr Sargant or by Pavlov himself, do we see anything that even looks like emotional abreaction. The abnormal behaviour of Pavlov's dogs was always the direct result of imposed stresses – *not* of the release or acting out of pent up emotion. To restore them after breakdown, Pavlov's dogs were never treated abreactively but were given simple sedation. The fact is that emotional abreaction simply will not fit in at all into the Pavlovian formula of breakdown under stress because it is psychologically and dynamically the exact opposite of such a process – it is the *recovery* from breakdown.

'. . . When we inquire what are the common features of both breakdown and recovery which lead Dr Sargant to see both processes as amenable to similar explanations, we find that both involve something which can be described as "collapse"; and both involve striking changes in behaviour. However, an examination of Dr Sargant's own evidence will show very clearly that the changes in behaviour involved in the two processes are exactly opposite; that in the respective contexts of breakdown and abreactive recovery, the word "collapse" means two entirely different things. . . . The collapse which super-

venes as a result of intolerable strain is a condition which
endures for some time and is manifest in breakdown,
restriction of personality, debilitating symptoms and
patterns of abnormal behaviour. . . . The collapse that
supervenes at the end of emotional abreaction is a
comparatively short-lived physical exhaustion resulting
from violent emotional discharge. It soon passes quite
spontaneously to be followed at once by healing, liberation
of personality and the disappearance of neurotic symptoms and abnormal behaviour patterns.'

Ramage is referring, in the last sentences above, to the
experience of the shell-shocked soldiers. He comments on
the fact that Sargant seems to link the violent emotional
experience of Pavlov's dogs in the flood serving to wipe out
all their carefully conditioned reflexes to the emotional
discharge of the soldiers which wiped out all their previous
neurotic symptoms, such as limb paralysis or tics. This,
Ramage says, implies that in Sargant's mind conditioned
reflexes and neurotic symptoms are essentially the same.

The soldiers' neurotic symptoms were developed as a
defence against facing up to what had happened to them in
their war experience. Once the experience had been brought
to the surface and the associated feelings expressed, the
neurotic defence system was no longer necessary. Pavlov's
dogs did not develop of their own free will the tendency to
salivate at the sound of a bell or to associate the sight of an
ellipse with a reward; they were taught to do so. The
conditioned behaviour was not a defence.

Ramage does not deny Sargant's thesis altogether. He
accepts that the imposition of intolerable stress can have the
effects he describes and can therefore be applied to the
brainwashing phenomenon. But cathartic emotional discharge leading to healing is something else – and that is what
is going on, he says, in therapeutic abreaction and religious
conversion experiences.

Not even Sargant has maintained that brainwashing or
sudden conversions necessarily last forever. He said:

'It is one thing to make the mind of a normal person break down under intolerable stress, eradicate old ideas and behaviour patterns and plant new ones in the vacant soil; it is quite another to make these new ideas take firm root.' The only way to do so, he says, is to consolidate the gains made. So Wesley, for instance, after winning converts at his emotional hell-fire sermons, quickly divided his new flock into groups which met at least once a week. Other preachers of his ilk who thought their work was done once conversion was achieved soon lost most of those they had so dramatically won for God.

An effective method of consolidating the ground won by political or religious conversion techniques is to maintain controlled fear and tension, says Sargant, and cites the Chinese Communist doctrine that wrong thought is as evil as wrong action. Such a doctrine would have the highly desirable outcome that most would not dare to question the rightness of what they have come to believe as that would clearly be wrong thought – and punishable, should the wrong thought slip out unintentionally in conversation or even in one's sleep.

Quite clearly brainwashing does not last forever – if it actually occurred in the first place – once the brainwashed individual ceases to be in the environment where the inculcated ideas are current. The American POWs who returned home did not retain Communist ideals: many, of course, may not have believed them in the first place but only collaborated to make life easier.

Lifton's subjects, once they reached Hong Kong, did not stay 'reformed' either but the psychological effects of the whole process were long-lasting. Most couldn't instantly adapt to Western life. It was as if, Lifton says, they had some psychological business to attend to, to re-enact what had happened and master it. Of course they also felt alienated in their new country as most of the Westerners had lived in China for very many years.

Years later, however, they were still grappling with powerful emotions and ideas implanted by the Communists, although hotly anti-Communist. Many still had fears of annihilation. But some claimed that they felt strengthened because they had had the experience of testing out their emotional limits in a way few of us are ever called on to do – and they survived.

Hinkle and Wolff say that even the most thorough brainwashing can wear off in a short period. Even those indoctrinated for five years could revert in a few months, once away from the environment.

As environment and the prevailing current of opinion have such bearing on whether brainwashing effects last, Brown comes to the conclusion that, as a technique for changing beliefs and behaviour, it isn't even necessary. Social forces alone will do the work.

'. . . The individual will accept a substitute belief *either* because it is capable of performing the same function as the old one – for example in satisfying the need for a totalist creed which provides certainty and controls his "bad" impulses – *or* because the belief has become orthodox and it is "natural" to conform, unless he is prepared to become a social outcast. Thus in a Communist community brainwashing is likely to work but is hardly necessary, since in the long run people tend to conform because they are social; but when applied to non-totalist individuals who are returning to a non-Communist society, it will not work at all.'

He does not, however, in this comforting dismissal, take account of so-called brainwashing techniques which may be applied within a society that allows the expression of various ideologies. Individuals who join cults are prepared to be social outcasts from the rest of society while conformists within their own group. Being a conformist and being a social outcast are therefore not mutually exclusive.

To dismiss brainwashing as ineffectual in the long term is to ignore the fact, as so far shown, that the social and psychological factors and unconscious conditioning which combine to create it may each be powerful influencing forces on their own. In all the foregoing accounts of the Korean brainwashing experience, all the ingredients are seen as roughly the same, only explanations differ.

1. The soldiers were forced to question beliefs they had never questioned. Their certainty was undermined.

2. Their behaviour was shaped by the use of rewards and other conditioning processes.

3. They were led to believe that no one at home cared what happened to them. They felt out of control and learned helplessness.

4. Degrading conditions and public humiliations served to undermine their egos.

5. They were forced to participate in their own indoctrination process by writing statements or organising camp activities.

6. Removal of their leaders left them without a clearly defined authority structure, and weakened group cohesion.

7. The Chinese, by pacing their demands and only making large requests after being granted small ones, imperceptibly won their commitment.

8. Need for friendship and approval led them to comply with their jailers.

9. Induced anxiety, guilt, fear and insecurity led to suggestibility and a need to confess.

10. The unpredictability of their captors' behaviour confused their expectations and assumptions. Without a 'norm' to which they could adapt, they felt even less in control.

None of these stressors is situation-specific. Although the effects were heightened by severe physical duress in Korea, each can be seen in operation in more ordinary everyday contexts. The next four chapters attempt to show how circumstances, conditioned responses, physical and emotional reactions can all act to weaken that which we choose to regard as the unassailable self. Rather than the prey of victimising external forces, we may, if anything, be victims of our own false conceptions of what constitutes individual integrity.

3 UNQUESTIONED BELIEFS

The soldiers were forced to question beliefs they had never questioned. Their certainty was undermined.

In *The Social Animal*, psychologist Elliot Aronson remarks:

> 'Often beliefs that we hold are never called into question; when they are not, it is relatively easy for us to lose sight of why we hold them. Thus, if subjected to severe attack, such beliefs may crumble.'

Many of the commentators on Korea pointed out that when a soldier was uncertain of his beliefs or uninformed of his facts, he was far more susceptible to influence. Robert Blake and Jane Mouton, who made a study of interpersonal influence which was published in *The Manipulation of Human Behaviour*, found from their own experiments that 'conversion' and 'conformity' occurred most often when people were expressing ideological attitudes that were not based in personal experience. They suggested that an individual, to resist interrogation, must be well informed of the relevant and necessary facts and their implications. (As mentioned in the previous chapter, many American soldiers were confused about the validity or otherwise of claims that the United States had been engaging in bacteriological warfare.) Meerlo has also said that soldiers needed self-confidence and the ability to think for themselves if they were to have the courage to reject emotionally pleasant reasoning that in fact lacked truth.

It has therefore been seen quite clearly that lack of information and not knowing why one holds certain beliefs can leave an individual on shifting ground. But there is a difference between the concepts 'information' and 'knowledge'. Investigating the facts brings information whereas knowing why one holds a belief does not necessarily bring knowledge. A belief is a belief because it *isn't* knowledge.

Unfortunately, every individual's upbringing helps to invest him with a set of beliefs which, adopted when too young to be questioned, often come to masquerade as knowledge. According to Hans Toch, the eloquent and insightful author of *The Social Psychology of Social Movements*, the combined effect of childhood indoctrination and the socialisation process, at its most successful and effective level, serves to blinker an individual to reality and create a dependence on a belief system – any belief system. He can take blacks or whites but not the shifting shades in between.

Indoctrination is an emotive word. Perhaps for most people it is most commonly associated with the rather blatant process of persuasion that goes on in totalitarian régimes or the systematised thinking encouraged in minority political groups or religious cults (that other people belong to) where slogans or catchwords, such as 'state control' or 'enlightenment' encapsulate central concepts. It has a bad flavour, a bad feel, implying that the indoctrinated person has taken on board the conclusions of others instead of coming to his or her own. It flies in the face of free thinking, the rational weighing up of arguments and all such ideals that we think we hold dear.

But indoctrination, defined at its simplest, means to imbue with a doctrine. To 'imbue' means to permeate or to saturate, implying a process that can be much more subtle than the repetitious reciting of approved slogans. As authors who have been concerned by the concepts of coercion and behaviour manipulation show, most of us are indoctrinated throughout our lives, often without even knowing it. Beliefs almost 'grow' into us. They are then sustained and protected, usually unconsciously, by the physiological and psychological processes of perception.

Hans Toch demonstrates with particular lucidity how indoctrination takes place in childhood, whether it is intended or not. He sees a child's vulnerability as fourfold. First and foremost, a young child has limited perceptions. *The world is his world* and his world is largely composed of his mother and father. As Toch says, in a world looked at through this particular lens, 'the most casual remarks of parents . . . can easily acquire the weight of infallibility'.

Secondly, a child is vulnerable because of his dependence. Very early on he will learn or sense that his needs are more likely to be met if he conforms to what is expected of him. If a child says something that fits with his parents' particular perspective, perhaps regarding the race or religion of the neighbours, he is likely to receive praise or approval that reinforces the 'rightness' of the view.

Humanistic psychologists believe that such conformity to the wishes of parents, in return for love, affection and approval, is the cause of much identity confusion later on. Carl Rogers, one of the founders of the humanistic movement, advocated the fostering of 'unconditional positive regard', that is, that a person should be made to feel valued for himself, regardless of what he does. Too many children grow up thinking that only if they suppress all their anger or weakness or become academic athletes will they warrant, and receive, love and affection. Intellectual awareness of the process, as adults, is often not enough in itself to overcome such deeply held childhood beliefs.

Thirdly, Toch stresses the restricted nature of a child's sources of information. As he points out, adults finding themselves in situations, such as in POW camps in Korea, where they cannot validate information, are more likely to succumb to propaganda and indoctrination than otherwise. How, then, can a child be protected from the effects of continual exposure to the views and behaviour of perhaps just two individuals – whom he idolises to begin with?

Finally, the process dubbed identification by the psychoanalysts plays its part in the insidious indoctrination process. The young child feels a need to model himself on his father or mother in order to find his own identity. To find clues as to how he should behave in the world, he picks up on the ways that his parents behave, particularly towards him.

He will note their reactions, their interreactions and un-wittingly imbibe their beliefs. A nod, an expression of interest, a puckered lip are all important pieces in a child's jigsaw. They cue him in to what is done and what isn't done, what is thought and what isn't thought. The parents are probably quite unaware that it is happening.

Sceptics might say that such parental power is relatively short-lasting. By the time the child is going to school, he or she is exposed to many different viewpoints and life-styles and is all too keen to ask questions. Toch acknow-ledges that – and has an answer.

'Early indoctrination,' he says, 'would be ineffectual if it were subsequently neutralised. Neutralisation, however, is rare because our society is constructed so as to provide every person with consecutive waves of relatively like-minded associates.'

The part of a town a child lives in (wealthy or poor) will dictate the school he goes to and the kind of children he meets there; the kind of school he goes to will dictate the academic progress he is likely to achieve and the further training he will take. All along the path, he is likely to meet more like-minded than un-like-minded people, all of whom will help to reinforce his unconsciously formed first world view.

In this way, Toch claims, socialisation supports early indoctrination. In most cases, all ensuing influences on a child serve to confirm rather than discredit. And even when children do seem to rebel, 'the deviations usually represent variations on pre-existing themes, rather than the elaboration of new ones'. The hippies of the 60s, perhaps one might say, smoked dope instead of drinking beer; ate meals sitting on the floor, serving themselves from a communal pot, instead of at a dinner table with place mats; sold jewellery or pottery on market stalls in-stead of entering business. Only the circumstances were changed.

As the psychoanalysts have shown, what we learn in our childhood doesn't always sit easily upon us. We are a mass

of contradictions, all too often manifested as neuroses. Toch
puts it this way:

> 'The typical product of socialisation is a person who has
> become incapable of accepting with equanimity the uncer-
> tainties and complexities of life. Instead he has learned to
> impose the beliefs of his parents on his encounters with the
> world. These beliefs provide structure where there fre-
> quently is none, offer certainty where there is ambiguity
> and predict events which are indeterminable.'

All is 'all right' unless the beliefs are put to the test. But if
doubts and ambiguities do force themselves upon the
attention, then they may have to be faced and old beliefs
rejected. But the belief that is least likely to die is the one that
something somewhere, some system, some philosophy, *does
offer the complete answer*. The unconscious indoctrination
of childhood may lead one to be susceptible to indoctrination
itself, whatever the doctrine.

So much for indoctrination that originates in the family,
albeit by the name of nurture. Just as few would cite the
family as a seat of indoctrination as such, so few people who
claim to be religious would consider that organised religions,
such as Christianity and Judaism, operate by indoctrination
either. Questioning is not prevented by any active means. It
might seemingly be encouraged, in order to further understanding. But the understanding that is achieved as a result is
not knowledge itself but the understanding that belief alone
can lead to knowledge.

Eric Hoffer, in *The True Believer*, links this to the fact that
all active mass movements, in which he includes religion,
rely on united action and self sacrifice:

> 'Self-sacrifice is an unreasonable act. It cannot be the end
> product of a process of probing and deliberating. All active
> mass movements strive, therefore, to interpose a fact-
> proof screen between the faithful and the realities of the
> world. They do this by claiming that the ultimate and
> absolute truth is already embodied in their doctrines and

that there is no truth nor certitude outside it. The facts on
which the true believer bases his conclusions must not be
derived from his experience or observation but from holy
writ.'

He sees our acceptance of 'not understanding' as governed
by our need for the certainty that Toch stresses so much. So
Hoffer says, 'We can be absolutely certain only about things
we do not understand. A doctrine that is understood is shorn
of its strength. Once we understand a thing, it is as if it had
originated in us.'

If we consider again Toch's four ingredients for childhood
indoctrination, we can see that our vulnerability to them
doesn't just disappear when we cease to be children.
Restricted access to information, for instance, can take many
forms and operates most strongly in organised religions.
Doctines cannot be verified, they must be believed – and of
course inability to accept this is what leads many people to
atheism. However, the power of early religious learning
doesn't disappear like magic if the doctrine itself is rejected.
In the West, Christian ideas of right and wrong permeate
most of daily life.

Similarly, the need to identify doesn't disappear, although
it is never as strong as it was in childhood. In adult life, we
make our judgements about whom we think worthy of
respect and, as a result, are far more likely to identify with
their ideas. Unconsciously we will want to give them
credence and adopt them as our own – an example of
behaviour that psychologist Leon Festinger called cognitive
dissonance, to be discussed in Chapter 6.

Conformity remains one of the requisites of civilised
society. If one wants to 'get on' in it, one has to conform to a
certain extent. Particularly in the professions, a need to
conform to existing views leads to indoctrination. In *Persuasion and Healing*, Jerome Frank describes the process
very vividly in the case of trainee psychoanalysts.

The would-be Freudian analyst has to start from the view
that Freud's thinking was correct. He esteems his teachers

and wants their good opinion. He puts considerable effort
into his training. If, *en route*, doubt creeps in, he is not in a
good position to voice them. He wants to keep the good
opinion of his teachers, he perhaps doesn't know enough yet
on which to base his opinion, but he has studied enough to
have made a psychological investment in his training and to
want to succeed. He doesn't just learn during his training, he
has to participate in it by undergoing analysis himself and his
training is not complete until he has produced the right kinds
of memories, thoughts and feelings. As psychologists have
shown (again see Chapter 6) participation in and repetition
of an action help to confirm one's belief in its validity. In the
case of the trainee analyst, any objections he makes to
interpretations made of his experiences or any refusal to offer
up significant thoughts and feelings is explained by his own
analyst as the time-honoured psychoanalytic stage called
resistance – the unconscious fight to keep all the hidden
secrets of the unconscious buried. Long silences, argumen-
tativeness, even too frequent escapes to the bathroom may all
constitute resistance. There is no way the sceptical trainee
can be 'right'. But if he carries on his training, his need to
believe in himself will lead him to internalise what he has
been taught and to use it as an escape route himself when he
has patients. Any patient who argues is resisting or transfer-
ring emotions on to him. Any patient who doesn't improve
was probably unsuitable for analysis. The doctrine protects
itself.

The first of Toch's four stages – limited perceptions – is
perhaps the most insidious in its effects. A child comes to
believe certain things because he doesn't see anything else.
Whereas the adult prevents himself seeing anything else in
order to carry on believing. In other words, indoctrination or
beliefs once established are constantly reinforced by what
psychologists call perceptual set: we tend to pick up only
information that we are 'set' to receive.

Why is it, for instance, that if we buy a new car or a new
coat, we are so often aware that a great many other people
also have the same model or style? Unless the phenomenon is

due to an unusually successful advertising campaign, it is in fact unlikely that there are more of such cars or coats around than usual. What has happened is that our attention has been drawn to them. We notice them now. That is perceptual set on its simplest level. But it is the same process that is working when we take in information that confirms our existing beliefs or ideas. If a person is committed to socialism, he is likely to pick up on articles, books and conversations that support his ideas and not so much ignore as be unaware of the content of much material or views that conflict. The ardent feminist is likely to be more highly 'set' to notice instances of male oppression than the, to her, occasional example of sexual fairness or even male subordination. The arch reactionary will see only wayward youth. The process has its basis in physiology. Our nervous systems would be over-loaded to the point of collapse if we were to react to every possible stimulus in the environment around us. We have to be selective. Unfortunately, we cease to realise that we *are* being selective.

We tend to cling tenaciously to our first impressions, even in the event of later information contradicting them – the primacy effect in psychological jargon. Similarly, a strong reaction to one aspect of a person's character or abilities may colour our judgement of the rest – the halo and horns effect. The male interviewer who, admiring the prospective new young secretary's long blonde hair, overlooks her poor typing speeds is an unwitting victim of the halo. The next candidate, who has excellent speeds but who also has glasses that remind the interviewer of his mother-in-law, is a victim of the horns. We unconsciously filter out information that we don't want to receive.

What these kinds of psychological concepts show is that all people tend to be rather more blinkered in thought than they imagine. It isn't, however, an immutable state of affairs but we do have to be *conscious* of the halo/horn effect, etc., in operation before we can counteract them – or put them to use. For instance, perceptual set can be turned to use in order to achieve what is popularly called 'positive thinking' –

picking up only positive information that can help one achieve a goal, instead of dwelling on negative possibilities that might thwart it.

One may perhaps take this idea of limited awareness even further, in relation to indoctrination. If indoctrination is the acceptance of a particular belief system or set of views without questioning or evaluation, it may be worth looking at just how much is regularly accepted in everyday life without questioning or exploration, in the hope that this may throw some light on why we *are* so vulnerable to influence of diverse kinds — while thinking that we have, in fact, made our own decisions: that is, the assumptions we all make — and some of which we have to make — about our world.

Jerome Frank calls our 'assumptive world' the order and regularity everyone has to impose on the vast amount of varying experiences that impinge on him, in order to function at all. From personal experience everyone learns to make a set of assumptions that enable him to predict how others will behave or what to expect from the environment. On the most basic level, we all start from the assumption that there will be a tomorrow, that we will wake up from sleep to a new day, and plan our lives accordingly. It is a practical and necessary assumption.

Other assumptions are much more personal. A child whose mother demands a high level of orderliness and cleanliness from him, reacts angrily if he makes a mess, approvingly if he tidies his toys, may assume that love is contingent upon his fulfilment of these functions. It is an assumption he may carry with him into adult life, enmeshed with innumerable other assumptions that colour his values and expectations.

As Frank points out, assumptions exist on differing levels of superficiality and duration — assumptions about the value of a particular evening class can be changed in accordance with the evidence of experience — and can also exist at differing levels of consciousness. Of the assumptive world Frank says:

'Only a minute part of it is in awareness at any one time and the relative accessibility to awareness of different aspects of it may differ greatly. A person may be clearly aware of his assumptions about the nuclear arms race, let us say, but be oblivious to his assumption that he must be perfect in order to gain his mother's love. Yet the latter conviction may have considerably more effect on his behaviour than the former.'

The framework of assumptions we each construct around our world is very precious – it acts as a kind of road map. If it is found that a particular set of assumptions does not correspond to reality, a disabling emotional upheaval is experienced. The assumptions have to be changed and that is not easy if they are deeply entrenched. But it is far more common, perhaps, to have one's personal assumptions pulled into question than for common assumptions to be exposed to contradiction. If it is the case that a whole group of people or a nation act on certain assumptions, those assumptions will probably gain the status of facts. As everyone believes them and acts on them, it is rare that they get called into question at all.

Collective assumptions that do have to change usually change because scientific enquiry has revealed that what was presumed to be a fact was in actuality a misconception. For instance, we now all know the earth is not flat. Where the evidence is incontrovertible, the assumption must be dropped. But it is far more difficult to dislodge assumptions we make about ourselves and our reactions, for we are into the realm of psychology here. We tend to think we can explain our own actions, even if we can't always claim to explain the mysteries of the universe. Psychologists who try to show that the reality of a situation is other than we would have expected are often up against a brick wall for they are tangling with intangibles.

But there are a number of attractive studies carried out by psychologists that show the degree to which we act on totally erroneous assumptions about our ability to make autonomous decisions and about the effects of our actions. I shall cite a few disparate examples.

We think we decide what we do

In the 1960s American psychologist Stanley Milgram ran a highly controversial and now much quoted experiment which investigated people's reactions to authority. He wanted to know whether, when asked to carry out a destructive act, but one condoned by a higher authority, people will comply or rebel. Or, more accurately, he wanted to find at what point people *would* rebel.

The experiment will be discussed more fully later but, in brief, the scenario was as follows. Volunteers of all ages and professions were invited, for a fee, to take part in a study supposedly about the effects of punishment on learning. Volunteers were paired as 'teacher' and 'learner' (although in fact the learner was an assistant of the experimenter). The teacher had to teach the learner a long list of word pairs. The learner, if he got one wrong when tested, was to receive an electric shock. The first time he made an incorrect reply, the shock was to be mild in intensity – fifteen volts. Every ensuing time that he made a mistake, the intensity was to increase, up to a maximum of 450 volts. The 'teachers' were told that the learner couldn't suffer physical harm.

Of course the learner was only seemingly wired up for shocks and didn't really receive any at all (although to convince the teachers of the genuine nature of the experiment, the experimenter gave each teacher a 45 volt shock just to show him how it felt). However, as the teacher sat 'operating' the switches on the equipment, the learner responded in a pre-arranged way: when supposedly receiving a 75 volt shock, he grunted in discomfort; at 120 volts, he complained; at 150 volts, he demanded to be released from the experiment; at 285 volts, he emitted an agonised scream and then nothing more was heard from him. As the learner was in an adjoining room, the teacher had no way of knowing what had happened to him.

About 300,000 volunteers were drawn for the experiment in all. Before the experiment began, psychiatrists were asked to predict how far the subjects would go and the consensus was that only the 'lunatic fringe' would go beyond 150 volts, the tenth of the 30 shock levels. The assumptions behind these predictions were, first, that people are for the most part decent and don't like hurting innocent others and, second, that a person is in command of his own behaviour and he *decides* what he will do.

To the amazement of Milgram and the psychiatrists alike, no less than 62 per cent of people tested continued to give shocks right up to the 450 volt level. As Milgram was careful to point out, his subjects were a good cross-section of an ordinary population, rather than sadists. Most suffered extreme stress while giving the shocks and afterwards couldn't believe they had been capable of doing such a thing.

What the assumptions of psychiatrists and experimenters alike had failed to take into account in this experiment was that the concept of duty and obedience towards a respected authority has a very deeply entrenched hold on people in general. As Milgram said in his book *Obedience to Authority*: 'This is perhaps the most fundamental lesson of our study: ordinary people simply doing their jobs and without any particular hostility on their part can become agents in a terrible destructive process.'

A very treasured assumption that only the few would ever be prevailed upon to carry out actions completely contrary to 'fundamental standards of morality' had to bite the dust. People do not make their own decisions based on their own, and collective, standards of behaviour *always*, because few have the resources to resist authority. Circumstances can affect our actions more dramatically than we could ever allow ourselves to believe. (A more detailed account of the experiment and findings appears in Chapter 6.)

Assumptions based on language

Assumptions may affect behaviour in very subtle ways. Benjamin Lee Whorf has shown that our assumptions about the meanings of words can actually have alarming effects on our actions. He discovered while working for a fire insurance company that many fires started not because of people's carelessness but because they misread the situation, due to their understanding of words commonly used to describe it. (Article in *Language, Culture and Personality*.) He found, for instance, that men working in the vicinity of a storage of gasoline drums were conscious of fire hazard and careful of their behaviour; but that, when around what were designated as 'empty gasoline drums', their actions might be different – unrestricted smoking and throwing down of stubs was quite common. Yet the empty drums are even more dangerous because they contain explosive vapour. Whorf suggests that the problem is people's normal understanding of the word 'empty'. Empty, to the men concerned, meant the drums were 'null', 'inert'. 'This is a general formula for the linguistic conditioning of behaviour into hazardous forms,' says Whorf.

Another example of language-induced hazardous behaviour that he cites occurred in a wood distillation plant where the metal stills were insulated with a substance called spun limestone. No effort was made by the workers to protect this covering from excessive heat or flame. When, eventually, the fire below one of the stills spread to the 'limestone', everyone was astounded to see that the limestone burned quite furiously. Because of exposure to acetic acid fumes from the stills, part of the limestone (calcium carbonate) had converted to calcium acetate, which, when heated by fire, formed inflammable acetone. Whorf suggests that the men in the works were misled into thinking the limestone covering was safe close to flame because of the name – limestone. 'Stone' implies non-combustability.

On the same principle, Whorf explained the accident that happened when a pile of 'scrap lead' was dumped near a coal melting pot used for lead reclaiming. Scrap lead was a misnomer, said Whorf, because it actually consisted of lead sheets of old radio condensers which still had paraffin between them. The paraffin blazed up and burned off half of the roof.

The label we give to objects and practices can therefore lead us to erroneous assumptions about the nature of those objects and practices.

Attributing reason to action

Despite Milgram's findings, we are deeply imbued with the idea that we are in control of our actions and that we know the reason for which we have done them. Psychoanalytic literature is full of examples that might disabuse us of this idea. For instance, what Freud termed 'defence mechanisms' is a fruitful area for study. When we are anxious about something we don't want to face, we employ a variety of cover-ups, which tend to be so effective that we really, consciously, do not realise that the motive for an action may be other than it appears to be. So the man who misses an important business meeting because he feels inadequate in the company of that particular group of associates tells himself that he opted not to go because he knows that such meetings are a waste of valuable time. Freud termed this rationalisation. Another defence mechanism, termed reaction formation, involves going overboard in an opposite direction in an effort to mask anxiety or guilt from oneself. A woman who finds the children of her neighbours irritating and unappealing may in fact pay them excessive attention, give them sweets, wave away even their grosser misdemeanours in order to hide from herself a deeply buried fear that she is unfeminine and unnatural for not adoring children.

While it would be very difficult to coax the man to admit he felt inadequate with his peers or the woman to admit that she disliked children – because they genuinely wouldn't realise it themselves – the tendency to impute some rational explanation to an action is more easy to observe in the case of hypnotised subjects who are given a command to do something at a given time after they have come out of hypnosis. Stage hypnotists often select something trivial, designed to amuse the audience, such as asking the subject to scratch his nose vigorously ten minutes after he has returned to his seat. To the delight of the audience, the unsuspecting subject rubs at his nose right on cue. But if asked why he did it, he might say unhesitatingly, 'Because my nose itched'.

Dr Bernard Diamond, professor of law and psychiatry at the University of California in Los Angeles and an expert hypnotist, hypnotised Sirhan Beshara Sirhan after the killing of Robert Kennedy. In one session, he asked Sirhan to climb the walls of his cell, and Sirhan obediently scrabbled to try to get up the wall. Asked afterwards why he had done such a thing, Sirhan said promptly that it was just a way to get exercise. Even when Diamond played the tape back to him, to show that Sirhan had performed because he was instructed to under hypnosis, the latter denied that that was the reason for his action. (*Operation Mind Control.*)

The self-prophecy quality of assumptions

Labels have a limiting function, both in the sense of drawing useful boundaries around categories to be defined and in creating boundaries where perhaps none naturally would have existed. If a teacher is told that a child is a slow learner, he or she then treats that child as a slow learner and the child is likely to become one, even if he was actually misjudged or incorrectly assessed in the first place. Labels limit expectations. The teacher by assuming that a child is a slow learner leads the child to absorb the given image of himself and also assume the image is a true one. Alarming studies from educational psychology have found that where teachers were told that half a group of children had a high IQ and half had a lower one, their own assessments of those children's performances tallied with the expectations they had gleaned from the test results – even though, in fact, the teachers had been given false results.

Unfortunately it is only when such experiments are carried out that the invalidity of assumptions based on such expectations come to light. In ordinary life situations, of course, the correctness of a label such as slow learner, anti-social, psychopath, seems to be borne out and confirmed by the fact that the individual so labelled proceeds to behave in the manner that others expect of him. Diane McGuinness, a psychologist at Stanford University, believes that the fact that so high a proportion of children designated dyslexic are boys, not girls (80 per cent), is related to inaccurate assumptions about the desired nature of primary education. A study of four-year-olds revealed that, when left to choose their own activities, girls spent longer on any one project than boys, and more often chose activities such as painting and stringing beads. Boys, on the other hand, opted for constructing three dimensional objects, were far more deft at such constructions than girls and were generally much more noisy and disruptive than the girls while at play.

McGuinness explains the variations by findings of the last decade concerning the specialised functions of the left and right hemispheres of the brain and the different speeds at which they mature in boys and girls. Boys develop their spatial skills first and they learn best by watching, manipulating and doing. Girls develop their verbal skills and fine motor skills first, making them better able to cope with learning to write and to draw and to listen. It is small wonder, says McGuinness that boys are so often noisy and difficult in class when classroom activities concentrate on teaching children the kind of skills that only girls are equipped to handle at that age and in the kind of way – sitting quietly in rows – that is inappropriate to boys' needs. Boys are forced to learn, in an atmosphere that is unproductive for them, the kinds of skills which they are not yet ready to learn. If they were left to develop their spatial skills first, they would learn verbal and fine motor skills in due course, when ready, without problem. But, instead, because they don't respond to the classroom curriculum, they are likely to be labelled dyslexic early on. And, if they are put in remedial classes to help them cope, thus confirming the diagnosis, they are well on the way to becoming dyslexic for real.

In effect McGuinness is saying that the assumption that boys and girls learn in the same way and develop in the same way intellectually is a prime cause of dyslexia. Until the introduction of more modern, free choice activity in primary schools, the whole of early education was based on this erroneous and all too far reaching assumption.

Assumptions based on appearance

In 1980 English psychologist Ray Bull published a study that had been designed to test the public's expectations about the appearance of law breakers. A group of 58 men and women, which included ten policemen, were asked to evaluate ten male faces as likely criminals, from photographs they were shown. The subjects had to say whether they thought the men shown were likely to have committed a mugging, rape, robbery with violence, taking and driving away a car, illegal possession of drugs, gross indecency or something other.

In fact none of the men were criminals of any kind. They had merely volunteered for the experiment. But one face was picked out 37 times as that of a likely mugger and two other faces were chosen 19 times as belonging to someone likely to have committed fraud or to have taken and driven away a car. One man was pinpointed 15 times as someone likely to have committed gross indecency. But no face was seen as specifically that of an arsonist, rapist or burglar. Overall, the policemen's choices were similar to those of the 'public'.

Ray Bull suggested that unconscious assumptions about the kind of person who would commit a crime might influence both police and witnesses. Police might less often suspect, catch or convict law breakers who didn't fit the required image; and witnesses to a crime, who didn't get a clear view, might be influenced by the power of the criminal stereotypes when asked to an identification parade (*Observer*, May 4, 1980).

Some studies *have* shown a link between criminality and appearance. Ray Bull suggests that, if that is so, it may be related to the way that people of unusual or unattractive appearance were treated as children. Unattractive children have been found to be punished more severely for misbehaviour than children who look appealing – which might lead the child to think, 'I might as well do something to *deserve* such a heavy punishment'. Similarly, jury studies have found that attractive defendants are more likely to 'get off' than those of less sympathetic appearance.

Examples such as these show how much of our behaviour is based on assumptions which are not based on fact. Some have adverse effects on the lives of other people, some serve only to deceive ourselves. To assume is to take for granted.

Rather than give up a firmly held assumption, there is often a tendency to opt for 'exceptions'. So Jews are very tight with money but Mr Goldstein round the corner is different. The saying that there is an exception to every rule allows one to continue applying the rule without questioning the exceptions and what their significance might be.

Assumptions are not facts, they are inferences that we act on. In scientific terms, a hypothesis is an assumption that something might be true but it remains a hypothesis until it is proven. It is merely a basis for reasoning, a position to start from. In ordinary life, however, assumptions are considered proven on very unreliable data. Twenty years of marriage to a selfish man and a couple of conversations with neighbouring wives may be sufficient to convince a particular woman that all men are congenitally inconsiderate and untrustworthy. Her assumption may be the basis for indoctrinating her own daughter with the same belief.

If beliefs and assumptions are not called into question or tested, we are unprotected against the upheaval that accompanies their disintegration if they do become subjected to attack. Nature is not alone in abhorring a vacuum. It is therefore, perhaps, unsurprising if sometimes a whole new belief system or a new set of baseless assumptions is gratefully adopted in place of the old.

4 CONDITIONING

Their behaviour was shaped by the use of rewards and other conditioning processes.

They were led to believe that no one at home cared what happened to them. They felt out of control and learned helplessness.

The unpredictability of their captors' behaviour confused their expectations and assumptions. Without a norm to which they could adapt, they felt even less in control.

Much has been written about the process called conditioning, its role as a therapeutic aid, its role as a coercive agent and the pervasive, often unrecognised, part it plays in the formation of attitudes, behaviour patterns and personality traits. It can be defined quite simply as a learned association between two things which consequently affects one's actions.

If a blast of air hits you in the eyes, you blink. That is a reflex action, an automatic response which takes place without your thinking about it or perhaps even being aware of it. Imagine this scenario, however. You are sitting in a doctor's surgery waiting room, right opposite the door to his room. Every time the door opens and he calls 'Next please', the blast of air makes you blink. You have a long wait and a lot of blasts of air in the eye. When you finally leave the surgery, you go to wait for a bus and, being first in the queue, are standing right in front of the doors as they open. A blast of air hits you in the eyes and in your head you instantly hear the words, 'Next please'. You have learned, temporarily at least, to make an association between doors that open and blast you with air and the words 'Next please'. That is conditioning, at one of its many levels.

The procedure known as classical conditioning developed from the work on reflex actions which Ivan Pavlov, the Russian physiologist, was carrying out in the early 1900s. He was not the first to note that reflex actions could be conditioned. In the middle of the nineteenth century, for instance, Claude Bernard noticed, while collecting gastric secretions from a horse for experimental purposes, that after he had been collecting the secretions for some while, he only had to enter the stable for the horse to start producing them. However, it was Pavlov who first paid the phenomenon more than passing interest, gave it a name and proceeded to make it the subject of his investigations. His work was totally concerned with the conditioning of reflex actions whereas his successors moved on to the application of conditioning principles to a whole range of behaviour other than reflex actions. For that reason, the process which Pavlov called conditioning is usually now termed 'classical conditioning' to distinguish it from what came later (operant conditioning).

Pavlov made his initial discovery much in the way that Bernard came upon his. He was engaged in studying digestion (for which he won the Nobel Prize in 1904) and had devised a way of measuring the amounts of fluid secreted in dogs' stomachs and mouths. The juices were secreted when he gave the dogs food, which was what he expected. What he didn't expect was what happened next. During the course of his experiments, he found that the dogs started salivating before they had even seen food, in fact as soon as Pavlov entered their room. It was clear that they had come to associate him with food and that association was sufficient to trigger a reflex reaction to food.

Pavlov set about investigating scientifically the ramifications of this casual discovery. Using a tube which carried saliva from the salivary gland through the dog's mouth into a measurement receptacle, he first measured the secretions produced when food powder was put in the dog's mouth. Then, taking care that there were no distractions, such as outside noise or movements, he started striking a tuning fork just before he gave the dog food. After he had carried on this practice for some time, he then tried striking the tuning fork and *not* providing food. The sound was sufficient to make the dog salivate almost exactly as much as when food was placed in its mouth.

In the jargon of conditioning, the food was an *unconditioned stimulus* and salivation to food an *unconditioned response* (i.e., food naturally and automatically elicits the response of salivation). The tone of the tuning fork was a *conditioned stimulus* and salivation on hearing the tone alone was a *conditioned response* (i.e., an unnatural response that could only be learned. No dog never previously exposed to a tuning fork would salivate at the sound of it. Only because a dog had been taught that a tuning fork signals food would the salivation response be set in motion).

That was just the beginning. Experiments were then carried out to establish just how long an interval between the giving of a conditioned stimulus and an unconditioned stimulus would still lead to a conditioned response when the conditioned stimulus was given alone. How long did the learned response of salivating to a tuning fork carry on occurring if, after a while, no food ever followed the hearing of the sound? Did the conditioned stimulus have to be something so blatant as the sound of a tuning fork or could it be something considerably more subtle?

It was soon discovered, for instance, that time was as sure a conditioner as sound or the sight of an object. If food was presented at very regular intervals (and no tuning fork struck), the dogs learned to associate the length of time that passed with the imminent arrival of food. They would start to salivate just before it was due. That is a phenomenon familiar in everyday life. Someone who is used to having breakfast at eight, lunch at twelve, tea and biscuits at four and dinner at seven thirty in the evening will feel hungry as those times approach because his body is conditioned to receive food on cue. Therefore the gastric juices start churning in readiness as the right time approaches.

But back to the tuning fork for a moment. Pavlov, having conditioned his dogs to salivate to the tone, wanted to know how permanent that response would be if food, which was the real reason for salivating to a tone, ceased to follow the tone ever again. He found, as might be expected, that as time went on and the dogs heard a tone but received no food shortly after, they salivated less and less to the sound of the tuning fork and finally ceased to salivate at all when they heard it. The association between tuning forks and food had been *extinguished*. However, occasionally, a while after the sound had ceased to produce any salivation, out of the blue a dog would suddenly salivate on hearing it. This Pavlov called *spontaneous recovery* and surmised that it meant the learned response had been suppressed rather than forgotten. But, as again no food would appear, the conditioned response would once again be suppressed or even become truly forgotten.

Another couple of findings from Pavlov's laboratory are worth studying before going on to see how conditioned responses of their various kinds can play a role, often unconscious, in ordinary human behaviour – and how our knowledge of conditioned responses can be used to *shape* behaviour.

Pavlov found that a dog which was conditioned to salivate on hearing a particular tone struck by the tuning fork also usually responded by salivating when it heard a tone that was either higher or lower than the original one it had learned by. Pavlov called this *generalisation*. Again, it is a phenomenon familiar in life. A woman who is attacked by a man when walking alone at night down a street may well come to fear any man who looms into view on any subsequent occasion when she is alone at night in a street. But Pavlov's dogs also showed the power to *discriminate*. A tone that was considerably higher or considerably lower than the original tone they had paired with food elicited far less salivation than one that was closer.

One of Pavlov's students found that discrimination could itself be conditioned. Using cards that showed a circle (followed by food) as a conditioned stimulus to trigger salivation, she found that the dogs would also salivate if she showed them cards with an ellipse. In other words, generalisation occurred. She then set about teaching them to distinguish between a circle and an ellipse by giving them food only after she had shown a circle but not after she had shown an ellipse. Once the dogs had caught on and only salivated to the circle, she proceeded to test how far their discriminative powers could go. She started showing them cards with ellipses that looked more and more like circles until, finally, the dogs failed to discriminate between them at all. What was most interesting, however, was what happened to the dogs while they were undergoing this experience. One dog, that Pavlov describes, started wriggling about in its experimental stand, tried to bite off the apparatus tubes and then, when taken out, began to bark violently and generally display all the symptoms of neurosis. Later testing showed that it could no longer discriminate even between simple circles and ellipses.

What had happened was that the stress of trying to discriminate between food and non-food signals (the circle and the elllipse) was too much for the dog. It was from here that Pavlov went on to study the neurosis that could be induced by giving a dog conflicting signals which threw it into confusion. (These findings were outlined in Chapter 2.) Pavlov's interest was to see how stress reactions affected conditioned learning. But it is relevant here to consider the Chinese Communists' tactics of switching from kindness to cruelty or the giving or withholding of rewards. They were inducing confusion and stress in prisoners by preventing them from learning to adapt to expected behaviour. As we shall see, conditioning which is a vital and natural form of learning that helps us function in our environment can become utterly disabling when it is maladaptive.

The conditioning of fear and anxiety, for instance, can be both adaptive and maladaptive – in other words, useful or disabling. A child who touches a boiling kettle and gets burned will learn not to touch boiling kettles again. A child who, having been burned by a boiling kettle, generalises its fear to all kettles, even when cold, has learned a response which ceases to be useful.

American psychologist John Watson is famous for his experiments in conditioning fear. He was an ardent enthusiast of Pavlov's ideas and is considered the father of behaviourism because he maintained that all behaviour, however complicated, is the result of learned responses to different stimuli. He thought that if one could find exactly which stimuli elicited which response, all the complexities of human behaviour would be unravelled, without any need to get bogged down in unmeasurables like ideas and emotions. In an experiment to show that emotions are only the result of simple conditioning, he set about to instil in a little boy called Albert a fear of white rats. Having given Albert an appealing little white rat to play with, which the child liked, Watson then started hitting a steel bar with a hammer every time Albert touched the rat. Startled by the noise, Albert soon learned to associate white rats with terrifying sudden sounds and developed a fear of the rat. The indefatigable Watson then proceeded to prove that Albert's fear had generalised to white furry objects, as he was just as frightened by the sight of a white fur coat and even Santa Claus whiskers.

Fear, however, is not a reflex action. It is a protective response that gets the body ready to react to a frightening or threatening situation. While Watson could show that it was just as easy to condition such emotional responses as it was to condition reflex actions, such as salivation, he found that emotional responses were not anywhere near as easy to extinguish. Ceasing to use the hammer and even verbal reassurances to Albert that the rat was harmless did nothing to reduce the boy's fear.

Conditioning that is maladaptive to our environment is not only produced by experimenters in laboratories with hypotheses to prove. Our experiences throughout life affect the way we adapt to all similar and not so similar situations. A man whose first two girl-friends were much more intelligent than he and who therefore made him feel uncomfortable, inadequate and anxious when he was with them, may learn to avoid too intelligent women in the future or he may generalise his fear and start feeling anxious in the presence of all women, whether emotionally involved with them or not. The latter response is patently maladaptive.

Watson thought that classical conditioning was the be-all and end-all of human behaviour. He was wrong in that. Certainly emotional responses to environmental stresses can be affected by many factors other than the particular stress itself. A psychologist called Liddell from Cornell University spent thirty years studying experimental neurosis, which is what had been induced in the dogs who couldn't discriminate between ellipses and circles. In one experiment in the 1950s, he exposed a mother sheep and her twin lambs to inescapable electric shocks. The mother and one lamb were in one room, the twin lamb in another on its own. The twin lambs had electrodes attached to them and every so often, as they roamed around their rooms, the lights were dimmed for ten seconds and then the lambs received a brief shock. Liddell found that the two lambs responded in very different ways. As the lone lamb became conditioned to the fact that when the lights dimmed, it would receive a shock, it started to act neurotically and ended up cowering in a corner. The other lamb continued wandering around the room regardless of impending shocks. It seemed that the mother's presence had a stabilising effect on that lamb which kept it relaxed and able to weather unpleasant shocks without becoming neurotic. One might generalise from this to the different effects that certain alarming experiences have on children who come from stable homes and children who live in an insecure home environment.

That is perhaps why psychoanalysts are sceptical of the behavioural approach to curing neurotic problems. The behaviourist believes that by teaching new responses a neurotic pattern may be made to disappear; the psycho-analyst thinks that the cause of the neurosis has to be extricated from the unconscious first, before it can be eliminated.

Behaviour therapy relies on the laws of conditioning. But, before looking at behaviour therapy in operation, it is necessary to discuss a second type of conditioning called *operant conditioning*, the potential of which was explored by American psychologist, B. F. Skinner.

Classical conditioning is concerned with responses. A tuning fork tone comes to elicit the response of salivation in a dog. A child takes its hand from the boiling kettle after it has been scalded. It is the tone or the burn that causes the reaction. Operant conditioning is concerned with behaviour that is initiated and that behaviour's resultant effects. Skinner believes, in line with his predecessor Thorndike, who said it first, that behaviour is shaped and maintained by its consequences. As a simple example, a woman who buys peaches from a particular market stall and on two occasions discovers afterwards that they are bad will most probably change the place where she buys her peaches. If, however, the peaches are consistently of excellent quality, she is likely to stick with the street vendor who sold them. Her original behaviour – going to that vendor – has been *reinforced* by its consequences – acquisition of good peaches.

Skinner used a variety of constructions and mazes and enlisted the aid of rats to prove his point. One construction was the 'Skinner box', a unit which released a food pellet when a lever was pushed. A rat was put in the box. In a rat-like way, it wandered around the box until accidentally it pushed the lever and received a food pellet. The rat ate it and carried on wandering about. On again accidentally pressing the lever, another pellet appeared. Gradually the rat narrowed down its field of activity so that the lever got pressed more often. Finally it made the association of lever and food and, whenever it was placed in the box, it headed straight for the lever. The consequence of receiving food reinforced the action of pressing the lever.

Positive and negative reinforcement are not always easy to distinguish. On a basic level it seems simple. A child who reads aloud a page from his reading book and then is given a sweet is encouraged to repeat the behaviour. The child who reads aloud and finds his mother wasn't even listening and certainly doesn't praise him is not encouraged to repeat the behaviour. However, why should it be the case that very often, in mental handicap hospitals, a child will repeatedly engage in destructive behaviour that only brings it punishment? The punishment would be expected to act as a negative reinforcer for the destructive behaviour. It is only now being realised that, in fact, the punishment is a positive reinforcer in this particular circumstance. For a child, locked in a room with countless other children, any attention from the staff is a desirable end. If the only way to get attention is to pull down curtains or knock things off a table, that is what the child will resort to.

As in classical conditioning, extinction of the behaviour pattern will occur if the reinforcements aren't forthcoming. But how quickly extinction occurs depends on how regularly reinforcement was forthcoming in the first place. The child who gets a sweet every time he reads aloud is likely to stop bothering very quickly if, on a couple of consecutive occasions, he doesn't get a sweet for his pains. If, however, his mother sometimes gave him a sweet when he read aloud but not always, he would carry on reading much longer after the rewards stopped because he would have no way of knowing the situation had changed.

Slot machines provide another example of these different kinds of reinforcement. A person who puts money in a chocolate vending machine expects chocolate every time. If a bar doesn't come out, he won't use that machine again, or will be wary of it. One-armed bandits, however, are another matter. Here the rewards for one's coins are intermittent. One is more likely to go on playing a broken one-armed bandit for longer than one would ply a broken chocolate machine with coins.

Using what he had learned about the power of reinforcements, Skinner found that he could *shape* quite complex behaviour in animals that was quite contrary to anything they would normally, instinctively, do. By offering reinforcements in the form of food he taught pigeons how to bowl. Using a marble as a ball, Skinner offered food each time the pigeons went near the marble, more food if the pigeons actually touched the marble, etc. Eventually he succeeded in conditioning the desired behaviour. Shaping of behaviour has been much used in work with the mentally handicapped, in order to encourage them to learn to lay a table or to get dressed alone. The reinforcement in question may be praise or affection.

Quite complex chains of behaviour have been conditioned in animals by the use of reinforcers. A famous rat called Barnabas was taught to climb a staircase when it received a certain signal (a light coming on), push down a drawbridge to cross to a platform where it climbed a ladder to pull a chain which brought a 'car' close enough for him to get in and pedal across a bridge, where it got out, climbed another stairway, ran through a tube, got into a lift and raised a flag which signalled the lift to go down to the ground. When the lift touched the ground, a buzzer went off and, by running to press a lever while the buzzer was sounding, Barnabas at last received a food pellet! Similarly complex but much more amazing chains can be conditioned in humans too, as we shall see.

However, all is not always plain sailing. Just as it was shown that reinforcements can be positive and negative for different reasons (and for different people. It was said in a previous chapter that the Chinese had to discover whether rewards or punishment had the desired effect on different prisoners), so natural behaviours can sometimes interfere with complex learned actions. Several researchers have found that animals trained to trade in a coin for a food reward may end up trying to eat the coin instead. One porpoise even died when it swallowed a baseball bat that had been associated with food.

Such hiccups notwithstanding, behaviour can clearly be manipulated by using what we know of conditioned learning. It can be manipulated consciously or unconsciously.

Behaviour therapy is about conscious manipulation of behaviour. It is based on the principle that maladaptive behaviour patterns, caused by faulty original conditioning, can be replaced by better, more functional ones. Suppose, for instance, that a mother brings her child for help to a clinical psychologist because the little girl has tremendous temper tantrums and screaming bouts whenever she is put to bed at night. What happens, she tells the psychologist, is that the girl is kissed goodnight and left in her room. As soon as she is alone, she starts to scream. After a while the noise becomes so ear-splitting that the mother fears for the child's safety – and the reactions of the neighbours – and so she goes to comfort the girl and try to coax her to sleep. The psychologist tells her that, unwittingly, she has conditioned the child to learn that cuddles and sympathy are the reward for making a terrible noise. The screaming behaviour has been reinforced by the fact that affection and attention are always eventually forthcoming. The reinforcement has to be extinguished.

The mother is told to ignore the girl's screams, no matter how long they go on. After a few nights, the child will cease to associate screaming with attention. Instead, she receives affection from her mother in the morning, the more affection the quicker she went to sleep the night before. A new, more desirable pattern of behaviour is then set up.

A behaviour therapy technique called *desensitisation* has been found effective for the treatment of many phobias. If a person suffers from severe agoraphobia, the therapist requires the patient to devise a list of situations that she finds frightening, working up from mildly alarming to utterly terrifying. Number one on the patient's 'hierarchy' might be walking down the front path; number ten might be shopping in a crowded supermarket. Having first taught the patient relaxation techniques, the therapist then takes her up the hierarchy, step by step, by accompanying her in each of the named situations or by asking her to imagine them. The patient is required to apply the relaxation techniques when she starts feeling anxious. What is happening here is that the patient is learning not to reinforce her fear by avoidance of the situation but by going through it and relaxing, to reinforce the realisation that, having walked to the gate or shopped in the supermarket, nothing terrible happens.

A similar technique is called *flooding*. Instead of gradually working through situational fears, the patient faces his worst fears all at once. The traumatic experience is repeated until the fears are overcome.

The most controversial form of behaviour therapy is *aversion* therapy where unpleasant associations are forged with the undesirable behaviours concerned. For instance, a paedophile may be shown slides of attractive young children while at the same time time receiving an electric shock. The idea is that the patient will eventually cease to associate young children with pleasurable sexual feelings. It is not a method that has had signal success in deterring deviants of any description and has incurred much outrage from those concerned by behaviour therapy's potential as an agent of control. Those psychologists who defend it claim that it can only be effective if the patient is motivated to change and therefore complies with the requirements of the treatment. Thus it is not coercion. However, some mental patients, it has been pointed out, may be 'motivated' to comply not because they want to change but because they fear their discharge date may depend on it.

Ethical factors aside, aversion therapy is not especially successful because it works by punishment, not reward, and punishment can often have undesired effects. A child who is punished for smoking may not stop smoking – as might be presumed if punishment were seen as effective negative reinforcement. Instead, he may just take care not to smoke where he can get caught. Or he may stop smoking but harbour deep resentment and hostility instead, which manifest themselves in other ways. As masochists may attest, those who have been punished by the cane at school have sometimes grown to associate punishment with sexual pleasure. And, as mentioned earlier, if punishment is the only source of attention a child can command, it can become a positive reinforcer for undesirable actions.

According to the principles of conditioning, behaviour is not learned when rewards are not forthcoming to reinforce it. Therefore ignoring bad attention-getting behaviour can be more effective than punishing it.

Skinner, the modern-day arch behaviourist, has been

accused of reducing human behaviour to a theory of cause and effect, a theory which, if not as simplistic as Watson's, still ignores the part that emotions play in governing people's actions. Skinner, however, does incorporate feelings into his theory. One feels confident, he says, because successful performance reinforces the expectation of successful performance. One feels happy because pleasant events act as reinforcement for happiness. One feels sad because of a lack of such reinforcements, such as attention from other people, success at work, etc. On a loftier level, acts of altruism occur because the honour and respect that accrue from them act as reinforcement for doing them – and therefore make them not altruistic at all. Different reinforcers work for different people. So one may commit a crime because money is what counts, another may be law abiding because respect is what counts.

Skinner's is an extreme view. But whatever one's perspective on the degree to which reinforcements condition behaviour, it is clear that conditioning does play a powerful part. Its effects are perhaps most long lasting when they are most unconscious. A prisoner in Korea would know his cooperation was being 'bought' if he was offered extra cigarettes or special privileges as a reward for going along with the enemy. He might be less likely to realise the power of a brief, unexpected smile or kind word from his jailer.

Blatant shaping of behaviour by rewards may condition a person not to perform the desired behaviour but to the expectation of reward itself. A *Psychology Today* article by Kenneth Goodall recounted how psychologists in Kansas tried to help a mother change the behaviour of her two daughters who regularly left their beds unmade, their clothes lying on the floor and their rooms generally in a mess. The girls agreed that they ought to change their behaviour so they cooperated in a system whereby they received a small amount of money every day that they tidied up after themselves and a bonus at the end of the week if they hadn't faulted on a single day. Their habits changed literally overnight. After two months of this system, they were told that they would get their money regardless of how they behaved. The conditioned 'tidy' behaviour again disappeared overnight and they reverted to sloppy ways.

In another experiment, a group of children who didn't like greens were rewarded for eating them at dinner time. A second group of greens-haters received no rewards, just admonishments to do what they were told. At the end of an arranged period, the first group ceased to be given rewards. They stopped eating greens. The second group ceased to be ordered to eat greens. They carried on eating them.

Sometimes other reinforcers may be stronger than the one that the psychologist is ardently trying to establish as the new basis for behaviour. Alcoholics who have gone dry during aversion therapy techniques have often been found to revert to old ways once they return to their old environment which reinforces the desirability of drinking.

Similarly, incentive schemes may not work if the reinforcement of money for working harder is less powerful than an existing reinforcement for not speeding up production. At the Western Electric Company near Chicago, fourteen men were engaged in attaching wires to switches for telephone equipment. Although the more units each man completed, the more he was paid, they never turned out more than a set number per day which was lower than the amount it was known to be possible to complete. Elton Mayo, the psychologist called in to investigate and suggest improvements for productivity, discovered that the men operated according to a group-determined norm of what constituted a fair day's work. If any one man exceeded the accepted quota, he was likely to incur the censure and suspicion of his workmates. The avoidance of such unwelcome social pressure was a more powerful reinforcer for maintaining existing productivity than was money for increasing it.

Deliberate attempts to alter behaviour by simple conditioning are obviously doomed to fail if more complex or deep-rooted human needs and drives are not taken into account.

Conditioning that is unconscious, however, is impossible to break if it remains unconscious. Once it is (or, rather, *if* it is) made conscious, entrenched responses or attitudes may still be very difficult to alter. They may be rejected on an intellectual level but still retain a strong hold emotionally. A good case in point arises from the women's movement, which has done much to question established perceptions of woman's role, to encourage escape from old habit patterns and to explore largely unexplored female potential.

Women in the feminist movement have for many years now focused attention on the fact that women have been conditioned to accept a role as home-maker and child-minder – a role that is still theirs even if they work a full week in employment, like their husbands; to put men's needs before their own; to devalue their own opinions and abilities; to accept that they can go less far up the promotional ladder and can expect less opportunities even to get on to the bottom rung; and much more. The past decade has seen a vast improvement in the options open to women, many, such as in the employment field, backed up by law. But much of the more personal, individual change has come about by women joining consciousness-raising groups where they learned to question numerous assumptions they had taken for granted about their lack of autonomy as people.

Particularly pertinent, perhaps, were discoveries that many common neurotic emotional reactions were due not to a fault lying in women's stars but in faulty conditioning. Those taught as children that it was unfeminine to express anger grew up learning to suppress any hostility that they felt towards their husbands either by letting it build up into a destructive underlying mass of resentment or by trying to dissipate it by displacement activities, such as compulsive eating. Those who were taught that men don't like women who are intelligent often fell into the 'fear of success' syndrome, so named by American psychologist Matine Horner who discovered in research that even the brightest female college students envisaged for themselves a future in which they didn't achieve academic success but stood down instead to help their boyfriend get through. Horner concluded that women were frightened that academic success would mean social failure and this seemed to be true also of women who came from achievement-oriented homes. The fear and confusion arising from such conditioning lead, according to Horner, to the desire to fail which 'comes from some deep psychological conviction that the consequences of failure will be satisfying'.

Much of modern-day psychotherapy, particularly approaches such as gestalt and encounter groups which enjoy more of a vogue in America than England, is concerned with cutting through the debilitating effects of such conditioning – for men and women. An approach which has been particularly supported by women's movement groups is assertiveness training – effectively, the art of not feeling guilty, developed by Andrew Salter in 1949. (More will be said of him later.) Women who have been conditioned to be passive and to deny their own feelings have been taught, by this role-playing method, that they do have the right to say no – particularly in the sexual arena where countless women have gone along with the belief that what the man wants is what the man gets.

Unconscious conditioning clearly has the power to shape personalities and change lives. Until it is called into question, it isn't even realised that conditioning has been the cause. Women just were less academically bright, less aggressive, less secure about their identities, less deserving of respect. And when it *is* discovered that associations between women and passivity are conditioned, rather than intrinsically true, the emotional break with that heritage is harder to effect than a purely intellectual one. Many women who work full time at responsible jobs and fully believe that their husbands or partners should play their part in home-running and family-rearing, still feel guilty if they don't see to traditional domestic matters or don't have a meal ready when the man gets home.

I have used women as an example of the power of conditioning, not because theirs is a special case but because, as women have started to fight against it, it is clear to see how difficult it is to drop in a moment behaviour entrenched over and well beyond every woman's lifetime.

Less immediately obvious as an example of faulty conditioning is long term depression, a syndrome which American psychologist Martin Seligman has termed 'learned helplessness'. He discovered the phenomenon in an unexpected fashion. He and his colleagues were testing a particular learning theory on dogs, which involved giving electric shocks to dogs that were strapped down and therefore couldn't avoid them. Later in the experiment, the dogs were put in open boxes from which they *could* escape, when given a shock, if they learned to jump over a barrier. But, to the researchers' surprise, the dogs made a cursory attempt to get away, by running round inside the box, and then instantly gave up, resigned to quiet whining while suffering the series of shocks.

Finally the researchers realised what had happened. The dogs were reacting to their previous experience of being strapped down and unable to escape the pain of the electric shocks. They had been totally unable to control what was happening to them. What they had learned, as a result, was that any actions of their own had no effect and that therefore they were helpless. That piece of learning was applied to any new situation too, even where they weren't helpless, as in the second box.

From this, Seligman came to see the same syndrome operating in people suffering from reactive depression, the type of depression that ensues as a reaction to some clear external stress, such as loss of a relative, or lover, or being sacked from a job. According to Seligman, people who suffer a series of such setbacks about which they can do nothing learn that they have no control over any of the events in their lives; that, whatever they do, things will turn out badly in the end. Therefore they give up trying. They see themselves as failures, and lose all motivation and interest in life, at the same time putting themselves down and wallowing in misery.

Seligman put his theory to the test. He subjected students to the unpleasant experience of being in a room where a loud, discordant sound was coming from a piece of equipment. No matter what knobs they turned, they couldn't turn it off – which was as the experimenter intended. On a later occasion, the students were waiting in another room where they did have the power to control the annoying drone coming from the equipment. But they didn't even bother to try.

The only way to help people who suffer 'learned helplessness' depression, says Seligman, is to concentrate on showing the depressive person that he *can* operate on his environment and be effectual – perhaps by giving him simple tasks in therapy at which he can succeed, develop confidence and then move on to harder ones. The aim is to break the conditioned conviction that nothing ever works.

Conditioned helplessness can perhaps be manifested as blunting of feeling. Writing in the *Daily Mail* on May 14, 1981 after Pope John Paul II was shot (shortly after a similar attempt had been made on President Reagan) Anthony Burgess said: 'That Pope John Paul II should be fired at and hit is no surprise, but there is something profoundly wrong with our age when we are no longer capable of such surprise.' Unfortunately, it might be the more amazing if we *were* capable of surprise when the events of the recent past, which include regular assassination attempts on American presidents and other people in positions of power or fame, condition us to associate such standing with possible violent death and desensitise us to it when it happens. 'That's what you must expect if you are a politician/pop star, etc.', people come to say, as though the threat of violent death were a natural concomitant of reaching public notice.

The point was made rather poignantly by *Observer* reporter Colin Smith after an air raid on Lebanon in July 1981, which left hundreds of people dead or wounded. Smith wrote:

'One father objected to my taking a photograph of his daughter, a girl of about eleven who had been brought in (to the Gaza hospital) with shrapnel wounds.

'"But the world must see what's happened," said the doctor whose name was Imad.

'"The world has seen these pictures a thousand times before," snapped the parent. "When did it ever stop anything?"' (*Observer*, July 19, 1981.)

While we unconsciously become desensitised to violence, we can still experience outrage at a programme that deliberately sets out to achieve that aim. In 1975 the *Sunday Times* published a story in which it was claimed that special units existed to train people to act as assassins. The reporter, Peter Watson, while researching his book, *War on the Mind*, had attended a NATO-sponsored conference on stress and anxiety. One speaker, Dr Thomas Narut from the US Naval Hospital at the NATO headquarters in Naples, spoke about coping with stress and, in the process, let slip that the techniques he had mentioned were being used with 'combat readiness units' designed to train people to cope with the stress of killing. Intrigued as to what this meant, Watson had two discussions with Narut from which he learned that Dr Narut was referring, when he said combat readiness unit, to the ordinary commando unit, and to naval men who were put into embassies abroad, ready to be called upon to kill, if required. He also said, Watson writes in *War on the Mind*, that men from military prisons were being selected to act as assassins in the embassies overseas.

The full story, as told to Watson, was as follows: Dr Narut's doctoral thesis had been concerned to discover whether particular films could provoke anxiety and whether that anxiety could be coped with more easily if a man was required to do some ordinary task while watching such a film. The work he subsequently did for the navy also concerned films but this time the aim was to find a way to induce servicemen who were not inclined to kill to be able to do so under certain conditions.

The method investigated was the screening of films which showed people being maimed or killed violently, with the aim of desensitising the men to such acts. Amongst the men selected by US naval psychologists for this training were convicted murderers from military prisons.

Watson described the so-called stress reduction training, as it was described to him:

'Men selected are taken for training to the Navy's hospital in Naples or to the Neuropsychiatric Laboratory in San Diego, California. The men are taught to shoot but also given a special type of "Clockwork Orange" training to quell any qualms they may have had about killing. It works like this. The men are shown a series of gruesome films, which get progressively more horrific. The trainee is forced to watch by having his head bolted in a clamp so he cannot turn away, and a special device keeps his eyelids open. One of the first films shows an African youth being crudely circumcised by fellow members of his tribe. No anaesthetic is used and the knife is obviously blunt. When the film is over the trainee is asked irrelevant questions such as "What was the motif on the handle of the knife?" or "How many people were holding the youth down?" In another, camera follows the movements of a man at work in a saw mill, slicing his way through planks of wood. The film shows his thrusting movements until he slips – and cuts his finger off. Physiological measures are taken to ensure that the men really do learn to remain calm while watching.'

Afterwards the men were shown films and given lectures in which people and customs in foreign countries whose interests might be counter to those of the USA were depicted in a biased sub-human light. The whole process took a few weeks.

The Pentagon denied the whole story.

Another example of conditioning at work may also illustrate that techniques consciously applied in the 'brainwashing' situation and therefore feared as something sinister and hitherto unknown, may occur quite unconsciously, with the same effects, in situations of ordinary life. The example is the conditioning power of words.

Perry London, in *Behaviour Control*, speaks of the 'semantic' generalisation effect in conditioning. We have already seen the generalisation effect, when a fear of white rats spreads to become a fear of all white furry objects. In semantic generalisation, the conditioned response also spreads to words. So a child who is taught to fear dogs may also come to fear the word 'dog'. In laboratory experiments, people have been taught, quite effectively, to salivate on hearing bland, uncontentious words such as 'style' or 'urn', where the word itself has been used as the conditioned stimulus. London suggests that it is possible, systematically, to give words and therefore language emotional connotations that are totally unrelated to their rational properties and meanings. He says:

> 'Love of God, of country, of tribe, of party or of principle; fear, distrust and contempt for strangers, minorities, majorities, races, religions, doggies and harmless little garter snakes – all have been taught in every human society by classical conditioning in which words take their connotations from the emotions aroused in connection with their use.'

Lifton also pointed out the connection between language and behaviour. Terms used in thought reform were never just words; they were all morally charged – either very good or very bad – and thus took on a mystical quality. As described in Chapter 3, Whorf showed that the carefulness or carelessness of behaviour around dangerous substances was dictated by men's understanding of the words used to describe them, and the associations those words had for them.

To return momentarily to the various protests of feminists, one common complaint is that we are all conditioned by language to see males as more significant than females. This occurs through the seemingly innocuous use of the word 'he' to describe an anonymous person who could be of either sex. For example: 'If anyone has an item to be added to the agenda, could he please submit it in writing.' Although it is known and accepted that, in such a case, 'he' is used in a generic sense, it is argued that it is the rare reader who will not visualise a male rather than a female when the word is read. The usage subtly reinforces existing conditioning that woman's role is inferior to that of men.

Jerome Frank, in *Persuasion and Healing*, expresses great interest in the power of conditioning words, both used consciously by someone whose aim is to persuade (e.g. an interrogator) and unconsciously by someone whose aim in fact is the exact opposite – to create an uncoercive atmosphere where expression can be free and uninhibited (e.g. a psychotherapist). Frank says:

'What would happen if the experimenter concealed from the subject both his own viewpoint and the fact that he was trying to get him to express it, but by using techniques of which the subject was unaware, caused the latter to say what the experimenter had in mind? One would expect this to be a powerful means of persuasion, since the subject would think that the viewpoint he expressed was really his own. Actually such a technique does exist and its implications for understanding aspects of psychotherapy may be far reaching, especially since psychotherapists use it continually, albeit unwittingly. A growing body of experimental findings, to which we now turn, suggests that a person can guide a speaker's verbal productions to a considerable degree by subtle cues of approval or disapproval without the speaker being aware of what is happening.'

Frank then goes on to discuss the experiments on humans which arose from Skinner's discovery of the technique called operant conditioning and described earlier in this chapter. If a pigeon could be made to bowl by having any 'bowling behaviour' rewarded by food, perhaps people's speech could also be conditioned in the same way, so that, by receiving rewards for saying the right thing, they would gradually come to say all that was wanted for the purpose in mind. The rewards, in the case of humans, would be signs of approval instead of food and the signs would have to be subtle, if the subject of the experiment was not to pick up on what was going on. Greenspoon published the findings of such an experiment in 1955. Some graduate students were asked to sit for about an hour and tell an experimenter all the words that came into their heads, which the experimenter then wrote down. The experimenter was ostensibly just the recorder of their outpourings. However, it had been arranged that he would attempt to exert a very subtle influence on the proceedings, unknown to the students. So every time one set of the students named a plural noun, he would make a grunting sound, with a slight affirmative inflection to the tone. When the other set of students named plural nouns, he did the opposite, producing a negative sounding grunt. Statistical analysis showed that affirmative grunts led the students who heard them to name more plural nouns and negative grunts reduced the number that were named.

Other experiments inspired by this one, and cited by Frank, showed that certain people are more susceptible to such conditioning than others. Anxious people, particularly keen to please an interviewer, however unconsciously, were more easy to condition than stable people. Compliant people, probably for the same reasons, were easier than defensive people. Dependence upon the experimenter's opinion therefore seemed to play a part in the ease or otherwise of conditioning by subtle verbal cues. It is worth pointing put that nearly all the subjects in these experiments showed no awareness that they were being conditioned in any way.

In *War on the Mind* Peter Watson describes the technique as one of the methods put into practice by police and security forces during interrogations. He describes it as follows:

'Using the technique of instrumental (operant) conditioning, a prisoner's behaviour may be modified by rewarding or punishing him according to principles laid down by the captors. These principles are not necessarily readily apparent to the captive. For example, a prisoner may be fed only when he talks about the general area in which the interrogators are interested. This way the prisoner "finds it easier" to talk about some topics rather than others. Every time the prisoner says something of which the guard approves, the guard says "right" or offers some form of encouragement. Gradually, imperceptibly, the field is narrowed down so that the prisoner is talking about what the guard wants.'

As Frank's main interest is in psychotherapy, he is more interested in showing how such tactics can have the same effects that Watson describes but without *either* party knowing consciously what is going on. He cites a study by Bandura in 1960 which showed that psychotherapists do have a tendency to register approval or disapproval of the statements their patients make, in accordance with their own personality traits. Twelve therapists were tested for their own ability to express hostility directly and for the extent to which they sought approval from other people. Afterwards, their performances in therapy with clients were monitored. It was found that those who could not express hostility themselves tended to react in a discouraging way if their patient expressed hostility. Those who had been rated as having a high need to be approved of by others also reacted against hostility from a patient. Therapists who could show hostility encouraged similar shows from their patients. The patients took their cues from their therapists' responses. Where hostility received disapproval of some kind, the patient used it far less; where it was approved, it occurred far more.

An even more indicative study by Murray concerned therapists who specialised in non-directive therapy, as devised by Carl Rogers. The aim here is for the therapist to convey nothing of his own views and reactions to what his client is saying but to provide simply a supportive audience for what the client wishes to express. Rogers' theory was that too many of our emotional reactions and behavioural traits are the result of conditioning in our childhood that it is 'right' to express and do only certain things. We adopt those expressions and actions that bring us the reward of love and attention from parents and suppress the rest. The positive regard in which we are held is therefore conditional on our right actions. The non-directive therapist's role was to provide 'unconditional positive regard', to exude warmth and caring for the client whatever he said or did.

Murray's experiment showed that it didn't work quite as easily as that. Sessions with patients were recorded and it was found afterwards that the experimenters could accurately predict exactly what the therapist approved and disapproved of, on the basis of the responses he made to information provided or feelings expressed by his client. His own attitudes were coming across loud and clear, despite his own belief that he had suspended all judgement. The clients were also shown to be affected by the shows of approval/ disapproval. They learned, over their series of sessions with their therapists, to offer up less and less disapproved-of material. More will be said on this topic in Chapter 9.

Frank warns against distorting the import of all these experiments. While suggesting that 'a technique of influence of which the person is unaware may be especially effective because he has no incentive to mobilise his resistance against it', he also sees as a limit on its effectiveness the fact that the reported findings 'apply only to what a patient says. The extent to which this corresponds to how he actually feels remains unknown. As with thought reform, it is important to keep in mind the distinction between compliance and internalisation. Operant conditioning clearly produces some degree of compliance but that is as far as one can safely go at present. It should be added, however, that one's attitudes are *probably* [my italics] affected by one's word.'

Psychological findings described in Chapter 6 will show that indeed they are.

Perry London believes that the power of conditioning techniques as a form of control should not be under-estimated. Both classical and operant conditioning have distinct parts to play. Classical conditioning can effectively control 'involuntary behavioural events' such as emotions, moods, sensations and the functioning of muscles, blood vessels and vital organs. Instrumental or operant conditioning, by systematic application, can be used to control voluntary behaviour. Both methods, he says, can independently influence various aspects of thinking and attitudes. They can also be combined (along with drugs, surgery or electronic machinery) to make it possible to teach almost any attitude, such as authoritarianism, any skill or any emotional disposition. He believes that while conditioning techniques have not yet achieved such a possibility, 'the potential for doing so is more evident than are any limitations on it'.

He gives an impressive list of the achievements to date of experimental conditioning techniques:

'A large body of scientific literature shows plainly that conditioning methods can be used to control several types of voluntary and involuntary activity affecting thinking, language, imagination, emotion, motivation, habits and skills. People can be conditioned to blush or otherwise react emotionally to meaningless words or phrases; to respond impassively to outrageous epithets; to hallucinate to signals; to feel fear, revulsion, embarrassment or arousal upon demand; to feel cold when they are being warmed; warmed or warm when being chilled; to become ill when lights are flashed; to narrow or enlarge their blood vessels or the pupils of their eyes; to feel like urinating with an empty bladder or not feel the need with a full one; to establish habits and mannerisms they had never known before; and to break free forever from lifelong patterns of activity they thought could never be forgotten.'

He describes some of these experiments and links the effects they produced to some similar effects found in ordinary life, without the assistance of laboratory procedures.

For instance, involuntary body processes could be successfully conditioned to such a degree that people who were trained to react physiologically in one way to a series of blue lights and in another way, physiologically, to a series of red lights shown in a certain order, were actually physically sick and developed severe headaches when shown the lights in a jumbled order. London says:

> 'The natural equivalents of these laboratory demon-strations are seen in psychosomatic illness and in even more common changes in bodily functions, ranging from diarrhoea to yawning, which are connected with a great variety of verbal and other informational stimulation. There is every reason to think the basic procedures involved are applicable to virtually every organ in the body and any expression of mood and emotion, with all the therapeutic possibilities that implies.'

But not all the effects of such conditioning may be therapeutic. London goes on:

> 'The techniques of breaking down established mean-ings, whether in propaganda campaigns or in eliciting confessions, are fundamentally the same as those des-cribed in the experiment where the subjects became ill – the rapid alternation of individually meaningful signals makes it increasingly hard to respond meaningfully. In propaganda, for example, the Nazis argued that the Jews were capitalists, Communists, democrats and tyrants, racist and mongrel, all at once, until the confusion of messages broke down the meanings of all these terms, leaving only one emotion-laden idea. Jews were bad . . . . Where the intent is to break down more profound meanings, as is necessary to get sincere false confessions, rapid meaningless stimulation is supplemented by anxiety and exhaustion until the victim, ready to forgo life itself for surcease of fear and for rest or sleep, takes leave of the last semblances of will. If the method works, he has now become highly suggestible and the new ideas can be implanted.'

That people could be conditioned to hallucinate to a signal emerged from an experiment instigated by Osake Naruse of the University of Kyoto. It combined classical conditioning with hypnosis to produce a weird and wonderful sensory phenomenon called 'conditioned hallucination'. A hypnotised subject was required to watch a blank screen. At a certain point, the experimenter sounded a bell or flashed a light and then projected, at a low illumination, an image on the screen. The image remained there only an instant. This was repeated. The subject was then given a sheet of paper and asked to draw several times the image he had seen. The experimenter then told him that he would forget the whole experiment and brought him out of hypnosis. In his normal state, the subject was asked to watch the screen again. When the bell sounded, or the light was flashed, nothing was projected on to the screen this time. But the subject, when asked to draw what he had 'seen' faithfully reproduced the previous image.

London also draws attention to the part that people's active participation can play in their own conditioning. One Russian experimenter, M. I. Lisina, could not get her subjects to constrict and dilate their blood vessels via the conditioning medium of electric shocks until she actually allowed her subjects to see their own vascular responses as they were being recorded. Then, understanding what the experimenter wanted, they were conditioned very quickly.

While the scientific debate will no doubt continue as to how far conditioning techniques can effectively – and lastingly – change behaviour, it can be seen that, taken in conjunction with certain elements of personality which can lead people albeit unwittingly to aid the conditioning process, conditioning is a formidable force indeed. Whether consciously applied, as in interrogation techniques, or unconsciously fashioned and absorbed from all that impinges daily upon our senses, it has the power to change behaviour, frame personalities and limit expectations. It can more easily be bred than broken.

5 THE INFLUENCING EFFECTS OF FEELINGS

Induced anxiety, guilt, fear and insecurity led to suggestibility and a need to confess.

Degrading conditions and public humiliations served to undermine their egos.

'Why,' asks Meerloo, 'is there in us so great an urge to be conditioned, the urge to learn, to imitate, to conform and to follow the pattern of family and group? This urge to be conditioned, to submit to the communal pattern and the family pattern must be related to man's dependency on parents and fellow men. Animals are not so dependent on one another. In the whole animal kingdom, man is one of the most helpless and naked beings.'

How man struggles his way to maturity is explored and explained in the now vast body of literature arising from developmental psychology and psychoanalytic thinking. Most of a child's early needs are similar to those of young animals; he is dependent on his mother for food, protection and warmth. But it takes much longer to learn to hold one's own and survive in a complex, thinking society, and therefore the child is dependent far longer on his parents and susceptible, far longer, to their conscious and unconscious influence.

He is, as he grows, testing out his environment, forming his identity, and using the reactions that meet his own actions to help him establish his potential and his limits as well as to form, and trust, assumptions based on them. He is learning to create a personal framework from within which he will operate as a member of society and he wants a secure base from which to move out and explore. That secure base is provided by the love and nurture that he can count on as a constant from his family but that love may be seen by him as conditional upon his obedience of certain ground rules.

American psychologist Carl Rogers believes that almost every child is the product of *conditional positive regard*. He learns to behave and express himself in ways that allow him to keep the approval of his parents. If his mother is angry when he shouts too much,or pushes him away if he asks for affection, he may learn to suppress his spontaneity or his desire to be held and touched in order to keep her good feelings towards him. He learns to subordinate his emotional needs to meet what he sees as the requirements of approval. As his world view is limited, he generalises or assumes that what is requisite for approval at home is also requisite for approval from society at large. Though his behaviour is shaped by these assumptions, his emotional *needs* don't disappear and may influence his behaviour in ways of which he is not conscious, as he no longer recognises that those needs exist.

Every child needs to know, in an alien and confusing world, what responses he can expect to different actions he may make, so that he can store the information and operate safely on the basis of it. He needs to know that he can take certain events and reactions for granted so that he can explore beyond them. And if he can't, he won't.

Psychologist Eric Erikson has plotted the psychosocial development of individuals from such a framework. He suggests that there are eight stages in the development of identity and only if the conflicts that arise at each stage are successfully resolved will the individual achieve a sense of secure identity. Stage 1 is *trust versus mistrust*: only if a mother meets the child's needs for attention, affection and sustenance will the child learn to trust other people. Stage 2 is *autonomy versus shame and doubt*: by the age of three, he is already exploring the world, as he knows it, and starting to act independently. If he receives encouragement from his parents, he learns to trust himself and his actions. If not, he learns to doubt himself and his abilities instead. At about age

four, the child enters Stage 3, *initiative versus guilt*: he is
now asking questions, coming up with his own ideas, making
up his own games. If his parents encourage him, he develops
confidence in himself. If they display impatience, he feels
guilty and learns to be wary of initiating activity for himself.
He may grow up to be dependent. Stage 4 Erikson calls
industry versus authority: the child, now at school, will
double his efforts to learn and achieve if he is encouraged and
praised by his teacher. But if he is always incurring
disapproval, he may feel he fails to meet others' standards
and learn to feel inferior instead. At twelve, he enters Stage
5, *identity versus role confusion*: now, at puberty, he finds
himself changing. If his identity has been positively reinforced up till then, he can weather the traumas of adolescence
but if he has been thwarted and made distrustful of himself
and his potential, it is a frightening period of identity crisis
and uncertainty. Only if he is secure in himself can he, later,
allow himself to be vulnerable to other people and to form
intimate relationships. If not, intimacy is threatening and
must be protected against (Stage 6, *intimacy versus isolation*). The two remaining stages occur in middle and old age,
when again changing circumstances may provoke identity
crises.

Erikson's stage theory provides an interesting account of
how and when insecurity may establish itself. The insecure
person, because he doesn't trust his own judgement, may go
overboard in trusting that of others. Because he is always
questioning his own worth, he is unlikely to feel confident
about making independent decisions.

Highly insecure people are perhaps the most vulnerable to
the wholehearted acceptance they find within cults because
their insecurity makes them distrust love on any lesser scale.
The insecure woman says, 'he couldn't possibly love *me*
because I am so worthless' and will unconsciously require
over-strong proof to convince her otherwise. Her demands
are therefore remarkably high, instead of low. Her conviction of her own worthlessness does not make her grateful for
any crumbs of affection she may receive but makes her

satisfied with nothing less than the whole cake, as proof of devotion. So, if her lover does not ring her four times a day, it is obvious he does not love her. He fails the test. Within a cult, love is offered twenty-four hours a day. Everyone is accepted as part of the 'family' and reinforcement of that acceptance is constant.

The insecure person needs to please because he wants to be liked. Having no sure conception of his own identity, he is dependent on others to shape it for him. He can form his own opinion of himself from that others hold of him. He may therefore put himself out to please others in ways that he doesn't really want because he fears losing their good opinion.

Parental power is now accepted as enormously influential in establishing a child's identity. When a child is very young, the world is peopled only by his immediate family and he learns to obey them because he has no other reference points. Because he wants affection and security, he is dependent on them and works to maintain their approval. In his search for models for himself, he imitates them. Not only are his actions conditioned (the stove burns, so he doesn't touch it again) but also his emotions. He may learn to fear being around anyone who is drunk because his father used to get drunk and then beat him and his mother. He may learn to suppress anger or to feel guilt or to avoid close contact, the influencing effects of which will be discussed.

As shown by Erikson, it is the reaction that a child receives to his early attempts to test out his world that shapes his later identity. If he is belittled at home or, publicly, at school, he grows to distrust himself. His ego is undermined. Similarly, an individual who finds himself in a relationship where he is continually being put down or overruled or treated harshly learns to lower his opinion of himself. The woman whose husband takes her for granted, expects her to wait on his every need and to sacrifice her own inclinations to his, but also to keep quiet when his friends are around and not show him up by her lack of intelligence, is unlikely to sustain a good opinion of herself. If she knows he thinks her inferior intellectually, she is likely to absorb that image of herself and act accordingly. She may have been conditioned that women don't show anger, women don't argue with men, women put men's wishes before their own, and therefore suppresses all her own feelings. But if she meets a person who treats her as if she were a real person, an attractive or interesting person, all her buried needs may surface and overwhelm her. She is his for the asking. Thus con-men part rich women from their wealth.

Frustration is a powerful force, whether it is the frustration that comes from being forced to be what one is not or that comes from dissatisfaction with what one is. Eric Hoffer, in *The True Believer*, describes how the latter can lead one towards the embrace of cosmic causes:

'There is apparently some connection between dissatisfaction with oneself and a proneness to credulity. The urge to escape our real self is also an urge to escape the rational and the obvious. The refusal to see ourselves as we are develops a distaste for facts and cold logic. There is no hope for the frustrated in the actual and the possible. Salvation can come to them only from the miraculous . . . they ask to be deceived.'

It has very commonly been noted that people who join cults are often those who are lost in life. Many who joined cults over the last decade were hippies in the decade before. Frustration with an imperfect world, run on greed and power and subjection of the poorest and weakest, and particularly precipitated by Vietnam, led to the rise in America of the hippie movement with its accent on peace and love. Frustration of those ideals led many to turn to religion as a source of hope.

A similar amorphous frustration with life led the Manson girls to join the Family. (See Chapter 7.) Scheflin and Opton described their background in *The Mind Manipulators*:

'There was a common denominator among the women who joined Manson's Family. They all felt alone and afraid in the world around them – essentially the world of their parents. They saw no comfortable niche in life for themselves and drifted from one life-style to its direct opposite while searching for something to believe in and something to belong to. They did not have clear identities in search of a place. Rather, they searched for a place to obtain an identity. Each came to view Manson as a healer, a father and a Messiah who would teach them to find their place in the world.'

People frustrated by illness or loss are susceptible to the powers of healers and spiritualists. They want to believe that things can be different or that the clock can be turned back, therefore, as Hoffer says, they are asking to be deceived.

Disillusionment with life may derive from unrealistic expectations – such as the perfect story book romance or the belief that it is easy to fall into the career of one's choice. But frustrated expectations of a realistic kind, such as earning enough to keep one's family clothed and fed, lead to a desperation that can make any offer of a solution uncritically appealing. Toch remarks wryly, 'A person may encounter problems because his parents have taught him to expect too much or because society fails to meet fair minimum demands. . . . Some persons would escape conversion only if they had no expectations and no demands at all.'

The solution to such frustration may be hate and the need to find others who can share that hate, making hate an acceptable end in itself: thus the conversion to a Hitler-type mass movement. Brown describes it this way, in *Techniques of Persuasion*:

'Psychologically speaking, what happens is that, when an individual is frustrated in his attempt to reach a goal, aggression naturally arises, probably with the original function of massing all his energies to overcome the obstacle. But when this cannot be done, the aggression must be turned in one or both of two directions: inwardly against the self or outwardly against a substitute object. Hence the frustrated person both hates himself and has the latent tendency to find external objects for his hatred, joining in comradeship with those who share his views. Anger is the great solvent of depression (which is self-hatred).'

Cults, such as the Moonies, seem to operate by manipulating the emotions of both hatred and love: hatred of all 'evil' which is represented by all outside the cult and love of all who hold the solution, all within the cult.

Relief from frustration is exactly what is offered by groups such as est (see page 190). Participants who are 'hung up' by the fact that their parents wanted them to be lawyers or that they have not yet achieved/acquired what they expected to achieve or acquire, may suddenly realise that they are trying to live up to standards imposed on them rather than following their own will. The relief of giving up trying and feeling *justified* in so doing is enormous.

Not everyone becomes converted to causes but many people join causes, be it a local political party, a church fund-raising group or an ecology society, because they are seeking relief from frustration. The cause itself is superficial. What is required is the social support, the attention and the sense of belonging which may have been denied them elsewhere.

The individual who suppresses or denies frustration may have no experience in coping with his emotions should they suddenly become aroused beyond his control. He therefore goes over the top. The catharsis achieved by the releasing of such emotions may take on an unwarranted significance and he casts about for reasons to explain them. Thus, at a revivalist meeting, he 'gets religion'. He does not know how else to interpret his feelings.

A senior psychologist at Broadmoor hospital classified 56 murderers by a well-validated personality inventory. He found that nearly half were over-controlled types, who had lived very conforming lives and had learned never to show hostile or aggressive tendencies. He concluded that because their normal response was to repress hostility, if circumstances arose such that they could not suppress their feelings any longer, they would commit extreme aggressive acts because they lacked internal cues for when to stop.

Many sexual murders are committed because of the suppressed emotion of guilt. So a man makes it his mission to kill prostitutes because they are dirty and disgusting and morally evil, but really it is because of his own unrecognised guilt feelings about sexual desire. Few people grow up to be murderers but most children are conditioned to feel sexual guilt. They are told not to touch themselves or their attention is abruptly directed to something else or subjects suddenly get changed, whenever they mention something sexual. It may never actually be said but somehow the feeling that sex is dirty or wrong or not to be discussed conveys itself to the child. The ensuing guilt, arising from any sexual enjoyment, may remain unfocused and therefore unidentified. Guilt feelings arouse anxiety. If the anxiety-inducing event is suppressed, the guilt and anxiety still remain but we cease to understand the reason we feel them.

Because guilt feelings are lurking somewhere below the surface of consciousness, most people are ready to assume guilt even when they are patently *not* guilty.

So, if a guest behaves rudely, a hostess may feel she is at fault. If someone receives no reply to a letter, it is rarely the recipient who is at fault for being lazy or forgetful, it is the sender who is convinced that he himself must have given offence.

Because people are so ready to assume guilt, guilt is an easy emotion to induce and to play upon. Because it is so often formless (the real cause being hidden from consciousness), it can be manipulated to take on any shape. Meerloo describes the process at work when confession is being extorted from a prisoner of war:

'To the horrors the accused victim suffers from without (physical duress) must be added the horrors from within. He is pursued by the unsteadiness of his own mind, which cannot always produce the same answers to a repeated question. As a human being with a conscience, he is pursued by possible hidden guilt feelings, however pious he may have been, that undermine his rational awareness of innocence. . . . The enemy knows that, far below the surface, human life is built up of inner contradictions. He uses this knowledge to defeat and confuse the brain-washee.'

The man knows he is guilty of *something*. He is guilty of having desires which conflict with the requirements of living in a civilised society or which conflict with the moral standards with which he has been imbued. The thought or action can be rationalised but not the guilt which remains pricking below the surface. Because he no longer remembers the why of the guilt, he assumes because he feels guilt, he must be guilty of that of which he stands accused.

The pervading sense of guilt leads to the desire for confession because that brings profound relief. Lifton describes the guilt/confession syndrome:

'People vary greatly in their susceptibilities to guilt and shame, depending on patterns developed in early life. But since guilt and shame are basic to human existence, this variation can be no more than a matter of degree. Each person is made vulnerable through his profound inner sensitivities to his own limitations and to his unfulfilled potential. . . .

'The cult of confession can offer the individual person meaningful psychological satisfactions in the continuing opportunity for emotional catharsis and for relief of suppressed guilt feelings, especially insofar as these are associated with self-punitive tendencies to get pleasure from personal degradation. More than this, the sharing of confession enthusiams can create an orgiastic sense of "oneness", of the most intense intimacy with fellow confessors and of the dissolution of self into the great flow of the Movement.'

That same orgiastic oneness manifests itself when confession takes place in encounter groups or groups such as est. Some of the feeling may be explained by the cognitive dissonance theory. (See Chapter 6.) The person who reveals his taboo sexual desires for his mother to a group of total strangers has to resolve the dilemma of 'I have just revealed my deepest guilt and fears which I could only ever tell to someone who was very close to me' and 'These people are strangers'. Therefore the strangers are now felt to be 'close'. Or such guilt feelings are unacceptable unless they are shared by others, in which case they become the norm. The people in the group derive support and validation for holding their own feelings by the fact that others have such feelings too. Many people feel a lifting of guilt if they realise that they are not 'alone' with their problem. The problem hasn't changed or vanished. It has just diminished as a problem.

Many people will open their hearts to strangers in pubs or on buses. Unburdening themselves brings them relief. It doesn't make the problem go away. But acknowledging it to someone else makes it more bearable because, in effect, they are saying, 'Tell me I am not such a terrible person for feeling the way I do.'

The skilled interrogator can play on people's need not to feel a terrible person. The totalist can stir up guilt about past behaviour and then plant the idea that such behaviour could only have been indulged in because the victim's ideology was wrong. By embracing the new ideology, he can absolve himself of guilt. Or the interpreter can confuse the victim as to the source of his guilt. The relief of confessing to the evil deeds of which he is accused of being guilty is equal to the relief he might have felt had he been able to confess to something of which he truly felt guilty, because what is being expressed is the built up pressure and the tension. As Sargant showed, he could get soldiers to abreact by encouraging them to 're-experience' imagined war horrors just as easily as when the experiences they relived were real. The emotion that was being discharged – fear, horror, guilt – was the same.

Society operates by the manipulation of guilt, by the setting of rules which induce guilt if broken. People feel guilty if they don't do a full day's work or if they don't pay sufficient attention to their children or if they don't do their duty by their parents. They may decide to break the rules but they can't decide not to suffer the guilt which can then be manipulated to ensure their compliance in some other, unrelated circumstance. As in the thinking of the psychologist who recommended toy manufacturers to play on working parents' guilt at neglecting their children to ensure the selling of more toys (by the giving of which parents could compensate for their shortcomings).

One of the earliest learning experiences for a child, which has long lasting emotional effects, is that a power outside of himself takes ultimate responsibility for his actions. If he reaches for a book on a shelf and in so doing pulls down fifty others on top of himself, someone else appears on the scene to save him. If he puts out a hand to pick up a bright object on a counter in a shop, someone makes him put it down. Judged by the findings of Milgram's 'obedience to authority' experiments (described fully in Chapter 6), it would seem that few people succeed in shaking free of the duty to obey authority figures and to think entirely for themselves. Parents, after all, are only the first in a chain of authority figures a child is subjected to. Society is based on authority figures. A child has to obey his school teacher if he wants to get on, the student has to obey the rules set by the examining authorities if he wants to get his degree, the adult has to obey his boss if he wants to keep, or improve, his job.

Because, as Milgram said, obedience brings rewards in our society structure, 'we come to expect *someone* to be in charge always'. So though a healthy parental attitude may equip a child to become confident, he may become confident of operating *within* the established system. And the system reinforces the early idea that he is never totally responsible for his actions, there is always someone else above to influence events. (Religion, after all, is based on such a concept.) The convention of the *deus ex machina* has long enjoyed a vogue in the theatre, not only perhaps because it eases the plot writer's task. It is comforting to believe that, when the going gets too rough, a policeman or a good fairy or a long-lost uncle will turn up to resolve the sticky predicament. Sartre's *Huis Clos* (or *No Exit*) had such shock value at the time because it depicted the conflict of three people for whom there was no one outside themselves to offer a resolution.

The belief that one is not in control can act as a self-fulfilling prophecy. Hinkle pointed out that people who feared, in interrogation conditions, that they could not hold out without sleep were the first to succumb to interrogation methods after sleep loss. And people who thought that hypnosis must be impossible to resist were the first to reveal all, when hypnotised, as they felt they could not be held responsible for their actions.

The willingness – or will – to abdicate personal responsibility, inculcated in us from childhood learning that someone else is always in control, is perhaps strengthened by the attractive illusion that irresponsibility means freedom.

Meerloo believes that it is fear of living, with all its in-built contradictions, that leads people to abdicate responsibility for their own lives. All the research findings show that those who seek to conform most or who join rigid-thinking organisations are those who can least tolerate ambiguity.

Meerloo, in *Mental Seduction and Menticide*, evocatively describes the dilemma:

'Living often seems beyond our power. Stepping out of a relatively safe childish dependence into freedom and responsibility is both hazardous and dangerous. Living demands activity and spontaneity; trial and error; sleeping and reawakening; competition and cooperation; adaptation and reorientation. Living involves manifold relationships, each of which has thousands of implications and complications. Living takes us away from the dream of being protected and demands that we expose our weaknesses and strengths daily to our fellow men, with all their hostilities as well as their affections.

'. . . Living requires mutuality of giving and taking.

Above all, to live is to love. And many people are afraid to take the responsibility of loving; of having an emotional investment in their fellow beings. They want only to *be* loved and to be protected; they are afraid of being hurt and rejected.

'It is important for us to realise that emphasis on conformity and the fear of spontaneous living can have an effect almost as devastating as the totalitarian's deliberate assault on the mind. . . . Trained into conformity the child may well grow up into an adult who welcomes with relief the authoritarian demands of a totalitarian leader. It is the welcome repetition of an old pattern that can be followed without investment of new emotional energy.'

As Milgram observed after the obedience experiments, we for the most part cannot handle total autonomy, nor total submission. Many psychoanalysts have noted that for most people, and for neurotic people most of all, it is difficult to be individual and 'confession' is one solution. Brown explains:

'There exists a "fear of freedom", of self-hood, which makes people want to submerge themselves in the mass and confession is one of the means by which they can do so, for thereby they lose those traits which cause them to feel separate. The other, of course, is to lose one's sense of personal identity by submerging it into the collective behaviour of the crowd.'

Toch is convinced that the inability to accept ambiguity in life is the precipitating factor in 'sudden conversions'. But such conversions only *appear* sudden, however; the processes leading up to them have been operating throughout life. Those processes are childhood indoctrination of ideas and socialisation, which keep the child, and now adult, within a framework of experiences where those original ideas receive least challenge. But eventually he may have to acknowledge that there *are* shades of grey between the black and the white of his convictions. Toch says:

'The typical product of socialisation is a person who has

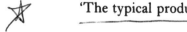

become incapable of accepting with equanimity the uncertainties and complexities of life. Instead he has learned to impose the beliefs of his parents on his encounters with the world. These beliefs provide structure where there frequently is none; offer certainty where there is ambiguity and predict events which are indeterminable.

'One consequence of our acquired predilection for absolutes is that it creates discontinuity in the way our beliefs change. We are forced to live with unrecognised doubts and hidden inconsistencies; we strain to preserve constancy; we assert convictions that we no longer unambiguously believe. Ultimately, when our reservations and hidden adjustments reach a bursting point, we merely substitute a new set of absolutes for the old. We experience the culmination of changes as a "switch" and we boast of a conversion.

'. . . The person must feel that "this time, the answer to all the problems of the universe is at hand". He cannot accept less because his specifications have always included complete certainty. . . .'

Eric Hoffer, in *The True Believer*, echoes such sentiments when he sees in the man who has just left the army the ideal convert to a cause. After the security of the army, the freedom from taking responsibility and the clear-cut routine from which no deviation was allowed, the free-for-all of civilian life is too much for him to cope with. He wants to be *given* reasons for doing things, he wants to be told that this or that is how it is and how it has to be.

Robert Assagioli, who studied under Freud and then parted company from his ideas and established his own school of psychological thought, called psychosynthesis, believed that neurosis was the result of an inability to make choices. He felt that Freud, with his theory of unconscious motivations, had destroyed the idea of individual will and that the person who acknowledged he *had* will was capable of becoming master of his destiny. If we are ambivalent about anything, he held, it was not because will was split but because there was a conflict between will and a confusion of drives and desires. Such a conflict was inevitable. All human life involves choices and neurosis was the product of trying to combine the incompatible instead of making choices. Totalism, perhaps, works by denying there are choices to be made.

Many authors have said that all mass movements are interchangeable and that the person who is suited to become a Fascist could as easily become a Communist because both organisations are equally authoritarian in approach. An experiment carried out by Canadian psychologist Thelma Coulter showed that Fascists and Communists shared a tendency not to be able to handle ambiguity. She found, from attendance at meetings of both, that they could not tolerate doubt or uncertainty and wanted decisions to be taken at once or actions to be instigated. Discussion they interpreted as criticism.

Crutchfield, an American psychologist, ran an experiment designed to test the personalities of those who were found to be high conformers. He discovered that they tended to be more anxious, more conventional in what they believed and how they behaved and dressed, more authoritarian and less capable of tolerating uncertainty and ambiguity than non-conformist types. He also found that they had lower self-esteem and less insight into their own motivations. They tended to describe themselves as 'obliging, optimistic, efficient, determined, patient and kind'.

It has been noted by those who have studied the characteristics of young people who joined cults (e.g. Dohrman) that the cultist is usually a person whose early life was spent in an oppressive religious atmosphere in an authoritarian home. He had therefore rejected one ideology for another, in the way that Toch described. The individual who has found a new set of absolutes must work hard, however, to keep them operational. The result, as described by Toch, can apply to any adherent of any life-cause:

'Beliefs, once adopted, become vested interests and are actively defended. Perceptual and cognitive mechanisms of various kinds "dispose" of facts and logic, so as to ensure that the world we encounter corresponds to our conception of it, rather than vice versa. . . .

'At a given point in the process, the believer has walled himself in. Every event he encounters must be processed in terms of his beliefs. Every opportunity must be used to cement his system. At this stage, only authority can produce innovation. Nothing remains of autonomy except the ingenuity exercised in the all-consuming enterprise of ensuring that real autonomy can never be regained.'

The argument against the concept of brainwashing is that people cannot be converted to believe something which is totally alien to them and the belief certainly cannot be sustained when the individual is back in an environment where that belief is not commonly held. However most conversions are in some part voluntary in that the convert is looking for something to believe. As has been shown, the beliefs, far from being alien, reinforce his own and fulfil his needs. A young man may be 'saved' from the Moonies and he may come to despise their teachings himself. He rejects the trappings but, unless he comes to question *why* he had believed instead of *what* he had believed, he may well continue to seek the absolute answer and accept it in different clothes.

There is a tendency to eulogise the 'gut reaction' or to imbue events with significance if they arouse emotions: 'As soon as I saw him, I felt this sense of peace' or 'when I heard his words I was suddenly deeply moved'. The experience of the emotion then justifies belief in whatever aroused it. As has, it is hoped, been shown, emotions can be aroused by many means and for many reasons other than what is immediately apparent.

As psychotherapists well know, many of the emotions that patients feel towards them are in fact emotions felt towards their parents/spouses or whomever and which were never expressed. Similarly when a man says to a woman he meets, 'You remind me of so and so', he often proceeds to react towards her as if she were the woman she called to mind.

Emotions may not be such trustworthy barometers for behaviour if the emotions aroused are emotions that belong to a past occasion instead of a present one. Thus, fear of rejection, experienced once, may colour all one's future encounters. And unconditional offers of acceptance may equally colour one's judgement.

Our need to seek pleasure and avoid pain makes us susceptible to the manipulation of both positive and negative emotions. What sounds simple and obvious in black and white is in fact complex and obscure when our motivations are successfully disguised from ourselves.

6 ATTITUDE INFLUENCE

*Removal of their leader left them without a clearly defined
authority structure and weakened group cohesion.*

*The Chinese, by pacing their demands and only making large
requests after being granted small ones, imperceptibly won
their commitment.*

*They were forced to participate in their own indoctrination
process by writing statements or organising camp activities.*

*Need for friendship and approval led them to comply with
their jailers.*

'If the ordinary human brain had not possessed a special
capacity of adaptation to an ever-changing environment –
building up ever-changing conditioned reflexes and patterns
of responses and submitting for the time being when further
resistance seemed useless – mankind would never have
survived to become the dominant animal. The person with
deficient powers of adaptation, and excessive rigidity in
behaviour or thought, is always in danger of breaking down,
entering a mental hospital or becoming a chronic neurotic.'
    So said William Sargant in *Battle for the Mind* and
although there are plenty of people prepared to take issue
with his particular version of the causes of mental illness
(notably psychiatrists such as Thomas Szasz and Ronald
Laing and their followers who maintain that the sickness is
within society and the 'insane' individual is in reality the only
real sane one, who won't adapt to that sickness) there is a
basic truth in the fact that the ability to adjust to a changing
environment is the secret of survival. Therefore, according
to Brown, in *Techniques of Persuasion*, it is far from
surprising that it is those designated statistically 'normal'
who are most likely to take on the attitudes that are prevalent

in their social milieu and to drop them in favour of others when the milieu changes.

In line with his own belief (described in Chapter 2) that all individuals have deeply entrenched attitudes derived from personal character traits and more superficial attitudes which are alterable according to current climate of opinion, Brown concludes that 'we are both more rigid and more malleable than has hitherto been supposed, rigid in our basic personality pattern and malleable (within certain limits determined by basic pattern) in our peripheral personality, whose various roles alter as we move from one group to another'. He commented that such 'normal' adaptation to group norms was a saving grace for some in Korea. So long as the morale of a group of prisoners remained intact, the Chinese were virtually powerless to influence it. They had to concentrate on breaking down the group.

While some attitude changes may be crucial for survival (a man who believes that his environment has been adversely affected by the invention of the motor car would not survive long if he attempted to ignore its existence, particularly when crossing roads), others may be maladaptive. If it is 'normal' to change attitudes, it is however considerably less advantageous to do so in some circumstances rather than others. But because we tend to believe in the concept of autonomy, we may not realise quite the degree to which our attitude changes or our behaviour are not the product of our own decision-making. Psychological research has revealed the power of forces that are way beyond normal conscious control, and yet which can have, in some instances, far-reaching, destructive effects.

An 'attitude' has been defined as having three component parts: affect, cognition and behaviour. The affective component refers to an individual's evaluation of, liking for or emotional response to a person, thing or concept. The cognitive component comprises his beliefs or knowledge about that person, thing or concept. The behavioural component covers the way he actually acts towards the person or thing or as a result of holding the concept. As

Zimbardo points out, in *Influencing Attitudes and Changing Behaviour*, any deliberate attempts made to change people's attitudes have to work on all three elements. A technique that affects one's emotional beliefs but not one's actions is not completely effective.

This chapter will look in detail at a number of the discoveries that have been made about attitude change and methods of influencing behaviour but it will concentrate on those areas where the influence is a subtle one and its effects on a person unconscious. While fully acknowledging that television or direct political appeals have influencing powers, that more overt form of influence is not under discussion here.

Obedience to authority

'A person who, with inner conviction, loathes stealing, killing and assault may find himself performing these acts with relative ease when commanded by authority. Behaviour that is unthinkable in an individual who is acting on his own may be executed without hesitation when carried out under orders. . .

'Facts of recent history and observation in daily life suggest that, for many people, obedience may be a deeply ingrained behaviour tendency, indeed a prepotent impulse overriding training or ethics, sympathy and moral conduct.'

Professor Stanley Milgram wrote these words in the introduction to *Obedience to Authority*, the published account of an experiment which left shock waves rippling throughout the world. He had discovered that thinking man does not always make decisions in a rational way, in fact, sometimes is totally incapable of it. Circumstances and deeply entrenched behaviour traits can radically affect right judgement.

Milgram's experiment involved 300,000 people in an attempt to find out whether punishment had advantageous effects on learning. Or that was what the subjects were told. In fact the real goal of the experiment was to find out about the behaviour of the subjects themselves in a particularly stressful situation.

Forty people took part in each experiment and each time volunteers were divided so that there would be 40 per cent working class, 40 per cent white collar and 20 per cent from professional classes, the age range from mid-twenties to mid-forties. The first series of experiments was carried out at Yale University where Milgram worked and the volunteers were solicited through local papers in New Haven, an incentive being that they would receive a fee for taking part.

Each volunteer was paired with another person, supposedly another volunteer but in reality a confederate of the experimenter. The real volunteer was to act as 'teacher' and the confederate as 'learner'. The teacher had to help the learner learn a long list of word pairs and then test his memory. If the learner got one wrong, he was to receive an electric shock which the teacher would deliver by pressing a switch on the shock generator in front of him (to which the learner was wired in another room). The intensity of the shocks ranged from fifteen to 450 volts and there were thirty switches in all. Every ensuing time the learner made a mistake, the shocks were to increase progressively in intensity. (The teachers were all given a sample 45 volt shock before beginning, so that their belief that the generator was actually switched on would be assured.) In fact, of course, the learner never received any shocks at all but he always responded in the following way: at 75 volts, he would grunt in discomfort; at 120 volts, he would complain; at 150, if anyone got that far, he would demand to be released from the experiment. At 285 he was to emit an agonised scream whereafter nothing would be heard from him again.

It was arranged among the experimenters that if a 'teacher' turned to an experimenter for guidance as to whether it was right to go on administering shocks or not, the experimenter could give four 'prods', only progressing from one prod to the next if the first was unsuccessful. The prods were: 1. 'Please go on.' 2. 'The experiment requires that you continue.' 3. 'It is absolutely essential that you continue.' 4. 'You have no other choice. You must go on.' If the subject was still resisting and objecting after the fourth prod, the experiment was to be terminated.

If the teacher was still carrying on with the experiment after the point where the learner had lapsed into ominous silence, he was to be instructed, should he seek guidance, to wait five seconds for a response from the learner and, if none was forthcoming, to carry on giving shocks in the same way as if the learner had answered wrongly. The teachers were all told that the shocks would be painful to the learner but couldn't inflict permanent damage.

Before the experiments started, psychiatrists were asked to predict how the teachers would react to the giving of painful electric shocks to a person to whom they could wish no harm, albeit in the 'interests' of science. The psychiatrists confidently predicted that none but the lunatic fringe would go beyond 150 volts, their assumption being that people for the most part are decent and don't willingly inflict hurt where patently undeserved and that a person makes his own decisions about what he sees as right and wrong and acts on them, regardless of what he is told to do.

The predictions, of course, were disastrously inaccurate. They focused on the individual as an autonomous unit, rather than the individual as someone affected by the nature of the situation he finds himself in. Over all the experiments, it was average for 25 out of 40 people to carry on to the end, administering 450 volt shocks to their innocent partner.

During the experiments, the teachers who obeyed instructions and carried on with the shocks quite clearly suffered distress, according to Milgram. Tension, sweating and trembling were pronounced. Quite obviously they were in conflict, yet they didn't do anything to bring themselves relief and so end the tension (i.e., halt the experiment). Milgram commented: 'There must be a competing drive, tendency or inhibition which precludes activation of the disobedient response.'

During interviews after the experiment with the over-wrought teachers, Milgram started to get some idea of why they had acted as they did and how they had personally tried to cope with what they were doing. (Most couldn't believe that they had been capable of acting as they had.)

Milgram found that politeness, a wish to keep their promise to help the experimenter and embarrassment at backing out all helped to prevent obedient subjects from taking any action to stop the experiment. He also made the following points to further explain their behaviour.

1. Adjustments started to take place in a subject's thinking which served to undermine his resolve to break from authority, reduce the strain he was under and help keep up his relationship with the experimenter. For instance, he would get immersed in the procedures of the experiment in order to lose sight of the ethical issues. And he would decide that he was not responsible for what was happening; he was, after all, just the agent of an external authority.

2. The subject didn't *lose* his moral sense. It was just that the morality that was uppermost was the need to live up to the expectations of authority, to carry out what he had freely undertaken, or, in short, to keep his word.

3. The subject might start to attribute an impersonal quality to what was going on. 'The Experiment' became an entity in itself, with an impersonal momentum of its own. The Experiment had got to go on. At that point, the subject had lost sight of the fact that an experiment is the creation of a man.

4. The subject would see his behaviour as part of the honourable pursuit for scientific truth. This helped to justify it.

5. It was common for a subject to alter his perceptions of the learner in order to justify the pain he had inflicted on him. The learner became unworthy, someone who was so stupid he 'deserved' to be shocked.

6. Some subjects said that they believed all along that the experiment was wrong and this belief somehow served to satisfy them that, ultimately, they were right-minded

about the whole thing. They didn't see that thought not translated into action was useless as a moral safeguard.

Very few of the subjects were unmoved by what they had been required to do during the experiment. Most, during the experiment, registered protests or pleas of some sort ('The man might be ill, is this really all right?') and yet still carried on.

Other experiments on the same theme but with minor alterations to the procedure added still more to Milgram's knowledge about the circumstances which lead to compliance.

Particularly alarming, for instance, was the outcome of one experiment during which the 'teachers' only had to read the word pairs from cards, while someone else (a confederate of the experimenter) did the shock administering. Here 37 out of 40 teachers went on right to the end of the experiment because they personally were not giving the shocks and could therefore, they felt, absolve themselves from responsibility. Milgram pointed out the terrifying implications of this in a society where modern organisations rarely have one person doing everything. Someone shuffles the papers while someone else pulls the trigger. The breaking up of labour into small specialised jobs prevents workers from seeing the whole situation in perspective, so each effectively 'yields' to authority by carrying out his own part.

Milgram also found that obedience to the commands of the 'authority' (the experimenter) diminished if the victim learner was in the same room as the teacher and was lowest of all if the teacher was required to place the learner's hand on a shock plate so that he could take the necessary punishment when he made a mistake. Obedience was highest of all if the learner was completely out of sight but it was still high if he was visible through a glass panel. (But most teachers tended to look away as they pressed the switch!) If the learner was out of the room, that also served to strengthen the relationship between experimenter and teacher, which the teacher was reluctant to break.

The personality of the experimenter had no effect on teachers' actions. He could be aggressive or non-aggressive and the outcomes were still the same. But what did make a difference was if the experimenter was out of the room, seemingly out of communication with what was going on inside. In those circumstances, teachers were likely to cheat and consistently administer lower voltage shocks than they were supposed to. In experiments where teachers could choose the voltage of shock they wanted to administer, the majority opted for the lowest. These behaviour traits told Milgram that the high shock-giving in the main experiment did *not* occur because here seemingly was an environment where hidden sadistic tendencies could, allowably, come to the fore.

Other findings were as follows:

Women are normally found to be more yielding to authority than men but also more anti-aggression. Yet, in experiments where women acted as teachers, they too went on with administering shocks, just as much as the men. The only difference was that they seemed to suffer more conflict.

In some experiments, the teacher would hear the learner arrange a kind of contract with the experimenter: 'You'll stop if I ask you to, right?' The experimenter would grunt in what sounded like agreement. Yet, when the learner begged later to be released, few subjects raised the 'contract' as a reason for stopping the test.

The authority of an individual has to be clearly perceived before the obedience factor comes into play. In experiments where the learner insisted that the experimenter do a trial run as learner first and the *experimenter* then went through the usual learner's performance of begging to be released, the teachers stopped the experiment despite the learner's insistence that they carry on. The learner did not have the authority of the experimenter, therefore his commands did not count.

Sometimes Milgram used two experimenters of equal status, one of whom wanted to stop the experiment midway, the other affecting to want to carry on. On such occasions, the teacher tended to stop because there was no clear authority structure for him to comply with. (Though some teachers did try to establish which of the two experimenters had the higher authority. When they failed, they stopped giving the shocks.) However, if, when there were two equal status experimenters involved, one offered to be the learner, his requests to be released were ignored. He had effectively relinquished his authority as far as the teachers were concerned. The other experimenter was seen as clearly in charge now and if he said carry on, the teacher carried on.

One final variation is worthy of mention. On some occasions Milgram set up the experiment so that three teachers were involved in the word testing at once, two of them being his confederates. First one confederate objected and backed out of the experiment, then the second followed. The real subject was ordered to continue his and their work. In 36 out of 40 cases, he would refuse to obey. In this situation he was conforming, rather than obeying. He needed to act in accordance with his peers.

Milgram believes that the ability of the ordinary, peace-loving, normally kind individual to obey commands to be cruel owes much to the fact that the need to be obedient is inculcated in people throughout their lives. Because parental control is part and parcel of youth, from a very young age, the genesis of our moral ideals is inseparable from the inculcation of obedient attitudes. To do well in school and then to fit into an organisation, obedience is required. Obedience brings rewards such as good records, privileges, promotion. We so much come to expect that someone will always be 'in charge' that the authority figure, whoever he is, does not need to exert that authority, just identify it.

Loyalty, duty and discipline, says Milgram, are terms that are saturated with moral meaning. The possession of such traits indicates nothing of the intrinsic goodness of an individual but the 'adequacy with which a subordinate performs his social role'. Having to turn against an authority figure means disruption of a well-established social structure and consequently creates embarrassment that most people cannot handle. Many find obedience the less painful alternative.

Milgram said: 'Although aggressive tendencies are part and parcel of human nature, they have hardly anything to do with the behaviour observed in the experiment. Nor do they have much to do with the destructive obedience of soldiers in war . . . or enveloping a Vietnamese village in searing napalm. The typical soldier kills because he is told to kill and he regards it as his duty to obey orders. The act of shocking the victim does not stem from destructive urges but from the fact that subjects have become integrated into a social structure and are unable to get out of it.'

That, to Milgram, is the more frightening. Aggression is easier to explain, easier to take steps to control. But the power of social structure to undermine valued moral codes is itself controlling. The result, as with Milgram's trembling, sweating subjects, is conflict but the need to obey seems to win. He comments wryly, 'We are not perfectly tailored for complete autonomy nor for total submission.'

Milgram's obedience experiment cannot be dismissed on the grounds that it was just one set of experiments after all. When the work was replicated in other countries, such as South Africa, Australia and Germany, the obedience factor was found to be even higher. A full 85 per cent of subjects complied with the experimenters. Psychologist Philip Zimbardo believes that the obedience factor was higher still in Milgram's experiment than superficially indicated. He wrote in a letter to the *American Psychologist* :

'The question to ask of Milgram's research is not [only] why did the majority of normal, average subjects behave in evil felonious ways but what did the disobeying minority do after they refused to continue to shock the poor soul who was so obviously in pain? Did they intervene, go to his aid, denounce the researcher, protest to higher authorities, etc.? No, even their disobedience was within the framework of "acceptability"; they stayed in their seats, "in their assigned place" politely, psychologically demurred and they waited to be dismissed by the authority. Using other measures of obedience in addition to "going all the way" on the shock generator, obedience to authority in Milgram's research was total.'

Some commentators have objected to Milgram's generalisation from his findings to the nature of war atrocities, saying that he is taking his conclusions too far. But is he? Sociologist Hannah Arendt, who covered Adolf Eichmann's trial, made the telling statement: 'The sad and very uncomfortable truth of the matter was that it was not his fanaticism but his very conscience that prompted [him] to adopt his uncompromising attitude.' Eichmann had said himself that he would have sent his own father to the gas chamber if ordered to. (From *Are We All Nazis?*)

Milgram's experiment caused a furore, not least because he was heavily criticised for exposing the poor subjects to such stress and suffering themselves. But the ethics of experimenters are not at issue here. Another, more low key experiment carried out by American sociologists, Sorokin and Boldyreff, shows the power that an authority figure can unwittingly wield in shaping others' opinions.

A piece of music (Brahms' First Symphony) was played twice to a group of over a thousand school and college students but the musicians were not identified. Although exactly the same gramophone record was in fact played twice, an expert introduced the first by saying that the rendering was far superior in beauty and feeling and technical excellence than the version they would hear next. The second was described, in introduction, as an 'exaggerated imitation of a well-known masterpiece'. Only 4 per cent of the listeners did not accept that they had heard two different pieces of music. Of the 96 per cent who didn't argue, nearly 60 per cent found the first piece superior to the second, 21 per cent didn't know and 16 per cent disagreed. A very low percentage therefore presumed to question the authority of the expert or to disagree with his learned opinion.

That obedience is so deeply entrenched is further illus-
trated by another experiment of Milgram's, this time
demonstrating just how difficult it is to breach social norms,
regardless of authority figures to reinforce them. Milgram
asked one of his students to go up to a person sitting on a
subway train and request that person to give up his seat to
him, *without* giving an explanation as to why. The student
was supposed to repeat this performance on twenty different
occasions and gauge the reactions of the people he asked. But
the student backed out before he had finished because, he
said, the assignment was one of the most difficult things he
had ever had to do in his life. So Milgram decided to take
over himself and he soon came to understand his student's
unexpected reaction. He approached a passenger on a train
and then found himself sweating before he could even speak.
When he finally forced out his request, he experienced
extreme panic. But the man did surrender his seat. In
Milgram's words:

> 'Taking the man's seat I was overwhelmed by the need to
> behave in a way that would justify my request. My head
> sank between my knees and I could feel my face blanching.
> I was not role-playing. I actually felt as if I were going to
> perish. As soon as I got off the train all tension disap-
> peared.' (*Psychology Today*, June 1975.)

When the rules have been set, we feel difficulty in
disobeying them unless we have massive peer support.
Which leads us on to the equally potent power of conformity.

Conformity

People cannot be trusted to say and do what they think is
right if others around them are expressing an opposite
opinion. The pull towards social conformity is far too strong.
That was the finding of psychologist Solomon Asch's now
celebrated study. He showed subjects a thick eight-inch line
drawn on one piece of card and asked them to say which of
three other lines on another piece of card was the same length

as the first. The other card showed a line that was obviously longer than the first, a line that was quite obviously shorter and a line that was clearly identical. But very few subjects chose the identical line! Asch had so arranged things that the test involved several 'subjects' at once, but only one subject was genuinely being tested. The others were confederates of the experimenter and all had been primed to give the same wrong answers. Asch found that his real subject, given the choice of sticking with his own judgement and being the odd one out or waiving his judgement and concurring with his co-subjects' clearly wrong answers, opted to do the latter thing and conform. Nearly three-quarters of his subjects showed some tendency to conform to the view expressed by the others in the room. In interviews afterwards, it was made quite clear by the subjects that they hadn't *believed* the chosen line was the same length as the first line.

In Asch's experiment, there were no penalties being meted out for being wrong, even so mild as a frown; so it is possible to infer that, in a situation where there might be some form of disapproval shown to a dissenter, conformity would be even higher.

Conformity was found to occur only if there was more than one confederate giving wrong answers. Similarly, when there were several confederates and one of them gave the correct answer, thus dissenting from his peers, the subject reverted to his own judgement and gave the correct answer too. Having one supporter was sufficient to eliminate the strong conformity drive.

Zimbardo suggests, in *Influencing Attitudes and Changing Behaviour*, that 'pressure toward uniformity may operate directly on opinions or indirectly by changing the way we perceive the world'. As an example he describes an experiment by Sherif that was based around the fact that a stationary light seen in the dark will appear to move, if there is nothing to judge it against. Sherif asked students the direction and distance that a stationary light appeared to them to move. This varied from individual to individual, some seeing small, limited movements, others lengthy, complicated movements. However, when all the students were gathered together to watch the light and to state what they saw, one after another, a group norm developed that fell between what any of the students, as individuals, had seen. Those who had described very small movements increased the movements they 'saw' and those who had seen the large sweeping movements reduced them.

The need to be one with a group, to have group approval and therefore social approval, means that individuals will very often change their attitudes *themselves*, to fit with the norm, instead of having to be persuaded. Just as an authority figure only needs to identify himself, not exert his influence, in order to command obedience, so a group may only have to be known to hold different views from a newcomer to that group for the newcomer to revise his own stands accordingly. The passive power exerted by social norms is all the stronger than overt power because it is bowed to unconsciously.

One reason for the strength of the drive to conform is that we tend to learn how to cope in unfamiliar social situations by following what others do. We pick up from others the accepted social code of behaviour for the circumstances we are in. Imitative behaviour is a process of learning. It can also become a habit.

Psychologist Irving Janis introduced a term which has now become a modern colloquialism: groupthink. He found that, in group decision making, the pressure for consensus is so strong that it can inhibit any expression of dissent. Particularly likely to succumb to the dangers of groupthink, he said, are tightly knit groups where morale is high. The enthusiasm of the members can lead to an illusion of invulnerability; whatever decision is made must be the right one because they made it. Any evidence that throws doubt on the validity of the course proposed is rationalised out of the equation. The group comes to believe in its own intrinsic morality, therefore there is no need to give consideration to any moral consequences of acts it proposes to carry out. The group decided it, therefore it is moral. In other words, the group comes to have a momentum of its own, fostered by the strength of seemingly united spirit. It is difficult for someone who has any reservations about the decision being made to put himself out of bounds of the inclusive bonds of the group.

Group norms can easily be established and adhered to even when the individuals who make up that group have no connection with each other, no common purpose and don't even know who each other are. 'Bystander behaviour' was first studied by John Darley and Bibb Latané after a now notorious incident hit the headlines in America. A woman was stabbed to death in the doorway to the building where she lived and 38 people witnessed the killing. The murder took half an hour and yet none of the onlookers came to her help or even summoned the police.

Latané and Darley carried out a large number of experiments using thousands of subjects to test out what it was that prevented people from coming forward to help in such emergencies. They concluded that the onlookers of the above mentioned murder were not callous or indifferent; they were caught up in a condition the researchers called 'crowd behaviour' where responsibility to act becomes diffuse.

They came to their conclusions from experimental findings such as the following. On a number of occasions a small number of students were asked to sit in a room and fill out some forms. The students didn't know each other. After a little while, smoke started billowing under the door. Only in 38 per cent of the student groups did at least one person get up to investigate. When a student was left alone in the room and saw smoke, in three-quarters of cases the student would get up and investigate within four minutes.

The researchers found that crowd behaviour didn't just apply when people in a group didn't know each other. A number of students were invited to bring two friends to take part in an experiment with them. Each trio were told to sit in a room and fill out questionnaires. While they were sitting there, they could hear the experimenter moving around in the next room. Suddenly there was a crash and they could hear her calling out in pain. The same scenario was repeated with just one student sitting in the room. The researchers found that there were half as many responses to the cry when people were with their friends than when they were alone.

Darley and Latané were led generally to conclude that when an individual is alone and an emergency occurs, he must act because there is no one else to take responsibility for him. If a child dies in a fire when there is only one adult with the child in the house, then that adult alone can be blamed for not saving the child. If, however, there are others present, responsibility doesn't fall clearly to one person and, as a consequence, none may take it. Each reinforces the other's inertia. Not-acting actually becomes the socially acceptable thing to do.

The need to conform in a variety of social situations, even if there are adverse implications for others outside it, is a strong one. Even if attitudes or beliefs remain unaltered, actions don't. But in many cases, where actions are in line with conformity, attitudes may as a result come to change too. More will be said of that in the next two sections.

Commitment

How does a person's behaviour affect not only his attitudes but also the very stuff from which attitudes are formed? In *The Psychology of Commitment*, Professor Charles Kiesler sets himself to find out, by describing his own and others' experiments which seem to provide some conclusive material to work from.

Freedman and Fraser found that if an individual wants someone to do him a big favour, the most successful technique for winning it is to induce him to do a small favour first. In their experiments, housewives were to be asked to place a large eyesore of a sign on their front lawns, urging passers-by to keep California beautiful. But first, half of the chosen housewives were asked to put a small unobtrusive sign in their windows. Those that had agreed to that request were far more likely to agree to stand the large sign in their garden (even if the two requests were made by, apparently, two totally unconnected people or even if the signs were about different issues) than those housewives who were approached with the large sign just out of the blue. The researchers concluded that the carrying out of the small favour led the housewives to see themselves in a new light – as 'doers'. Therefore the larger request was seen more favourably by them because they were already established in an active role. Quite clearly the actions affected attitude.

In his own work, Kiesler discovered the power of what he termed the 'boomerang effect': if a person has committed himself to something and is then attacked for his position, he increases his commitment, even if it was not at all strong in the first place. To test his theory, he asked a group of liberal-minded women to give out leaflets in favour of birth control to children at local schools. The next day, half of the leaflet distributor group received a leaflet themselves through the post, only this leaflet virulently attacked the giving of birth control information in schools. Afterwards all the women who had been involved in the original distribution plus others in the neighbourhood who were equally liberal-minded about contraception received a visit from a person, supposedly from the birth control campaign, asking them if they would be willing to give more active help in any of several ways. The women who had given out the leaflets and then had received a communication through the post attacking their position were far more willing to join up with the campaign than those who had simply given out leaflets or who had done nothing at all. Kiesler said, in general conclusion:

'The boomerang effect leads one to interesting possibilities . . . [and] might be related to the question of how people become more extreme in their attitudes. A committed subject might become more extreme under attack in an attempt to justify his past behaviour, since the alternative of abandoning his opinion to agree with the counter-communication is relatively closed. Since the process of self-justification may not be simple, the person might seek out others who are even more extreme as social support for his previous behaviour: perhaps even seeking other behaviours to perform that would justify his own. If so, one might turn a moderate into an extremist in a simple but non-obvious manner. First, induce him to perform some behaviour consistent with his beliefs and get him committed to it. Next, attack the attitude in question. We suggest that the person may be more amenable to requests for other extreme behaviour, more willing to interact with others holding an extreme opinion on the issue, and end up by becoming more extreme himself. Of course, the effect should depend on a particular combination of degree of commitment and strength of attack. That is, the degree of commitment should be high enough so that the subject can't really change his position and the attack should be strong enough to arouse the person's defences (but not so strong that he is forced to abandon his position).'

It is interesting that Hans Toch, in *The Social Psychology of Social Movements*, succinctly makes a very similar observation: 'Most of us underestimate the extent to which "extreme personalities" can be the products of personal commitment.'

Clearly we may have to alter a treasured concept of what commitment is. More usually people tend to see 'commitment' as something very personal, emanating from within. Psychological research would show that it can actually be engendered and manoeuvred from without.

In a study of the effect of forewarning on commitment, Kiesler and Kiesler gave a group of students an article to read, on a topic about which the students' opinions were known. Some of the students received a version of the article which had a footnote on page 1, drawing their attention to the fact that the content was designed to change their current opinion. Others had the footnote at the end of the article.

The remainder had no footnote on their article at all. Afterwards, all these students, plus some others who had not even read the article, discussed their views on the topic concerned. Those who had been 'forewarned' by reading the footnote before they read the article and therefore knew their views were under attack, were the strongest in holding to their own original opinion. So, says Kiesler, forewarning of attack may strengthen commitment if the commitment is firm enough.

This finding, borne out by many other independent researchers, may perhaps be seen in the case of religious cult converts who are constantly warned of the dangers of being caught by a deprogrammer who will try to overturn their belief, thus strengthening the converts' resolve to hold firm to their faith in the face of any evil.

Kiesler makes two other points worthy of mention here. He found, in an experiment carried out with researchers Zanna and DeSalvo, that if people committed themselves to attend a certain number of sessions of a group and then discovered that their own views were rather at variance with those of that group, gradually their own views would grow closer to the group norm. The reason here being, not that the individual concerned was frightened of seeming out of things but that, because he had committed himself to spending time with the group, he had to justify that decision. (More will be said of this in the next section.) Kiesler actually makes the comparison between this effect and the friendship that often grew up between POWs in Korea and their warders. It was, after all, the warders that the prisoners were 'committed' to relate to for the immediate or even longer term future, whereas other prisoners could disappear tomorrow.

Finally Kiesler comments on the fact that individuals seem to need to believe that their own actions are self-instigated, whatever the circumstances – a deception which may well arise because of an attack on one's freedom. Kiesler reports:

'. . . When one's environment is effectively controlled by

outside forces, then acting as if one's behaviour was really self-derived is one of the few alternatives left open. In my own experience (in a military training camp for recruits) I have found the percentage of recruits displaying hyper-military type behaviour quite large. That is, people behaved in a military fashion even when it was not demanded nor suggested.' [He gives as an example soldiers who regularly marched from their bunks to the bathroom or who saluted other recruits.] 'In behaving the same way in freer settings, one retains the perception of choice or self-responsibility in more prescribed situations.'

In effect, therefore, in rebellion against coerced behaviour, an individual may be likely to adopt that very behaviour to extremes, to make believe it was his own, chosen by himself. In the Patty Hearst case, to be described in Chapter 7, one of the main objections to claims that she had been brainwashed into acting with the revolutionary group that captured her was that she actually stayed true to the group's ideals for sixteen months after the majority of the 'army' had been killed and she herself was living apart from the rest. No one suggested that any mental process such as Kiesler has just described was the motivation for her actions – a need to believe, perhaps, that she had gone along with what had happened to her because such a life-style was really her own choice. The complexities of commitment and reactions against induced commitment should not perhaps be too lightly dismissed in such a context.

Resistance against the overt efforts of someone else to change one's opinion may lead to the very opinion change being sought, as Zimbardo shows. The idea, for the person attempting the influence, is to get the other to react against what he is being told but to so arrange things that what the person is reacting against is in fact what he really believes. As Zimbardo puts it: 'Reactance can be used in an ingenious way to get the person to disagree with statements that he or she would ordinarily agree with and to agree with statements that were previously disagreed with.' The would-be influencer makes statements such as 'You would have to agree that . . .' or 'There is surely no question but . . .' and the view he then puts up is the view he is aiming to put down. So the committee member who wants the club outing to be arranged by train rather than by coach, says, 'Well, you must agree that coaches are a more pleasant way to travel. You can see the countryside.' The other committee member, who really prefers coach travel, may be stung to say, 'Oh no, they are not' because he resents being cornered and having it implied that there is no room for opinion on the matter.

Jack Brehm, the author of reactance theory, describes it as follows: 'the perception that a communication is attempting to influence will tend to be seen as a threat to one's freedom to decide for oneself.' Here again, therefore, illusions of autonomy and self-motivation can lead people to be most prey to the influence of others.

Cognitive dissonance

Why should actions so often shape our attitudes, rather than vice versa? Much may be explained by Leon Festinger's cognitive dissonance theory, whereby people tend to search for justifications to reduce the tension created by holding two inconsistent attitudes or performing an act inconsistent with an attitude. On the simplest level, if a woman is choosing an evening dress and is undecided between a long blue one and a knee-length black one, whichever she eventually chooses, she will have to justify her choice to herself. She decides on the black one and tells herself that the blue one would have been impractical anyway. If she had chosen the blue one, she would probably convince herself that the black one wasn't dressy enough. She needs to reduce the tension caused by the fact that she liked both but could only have one. Therefore one had to be more right than the other.

That is cognitive dissonance at its most basic – and reasonable. But behaviour based on the need to reduce dissonance can be far more subtle to detect and alarming in its outcome.

Festinger proved the point when he studied the effects of cognitive dissonance on the beliefs of a small religious cult. The leader, Mrs Keech, claimed that she received messages from beings on another planet and that she had been informed that an earthquake and flood would signal the end of the world one day in December. But those who had been committed to Mrs Keech would be saved by a spaceship the night before. On the appointed night, the followers waited anxiously for the spaceship and of course it didn't come. Festinger was there because he was interested to see how the devoted followers would cope with the tension that would result from having believed and committed themselves to belief and then being proved wrong. The group was highly upset when midnight came and went with no sight of a spaceship. But then Mrs Keech claimed to have received a message saying that the devotion of her and her followers had been sufficient to avert the impending disaster. The followers were then able to esteem Mrs Keech again and continue their belief in her. Moreover, whereas before they had eschewed publicity, they now actively sought it, in an effort to win more people over to their cause.

If Mrs Keech's followers had not heard the message, they would have had to see themselves as fools for believing her. They would have been of less worth as individuals. Therefore, whatever the belief, they would have seized on any way to continue to hold it that would satisfy their need for consistent behaviour on their own part and for respecting themselves. In the same way, many devotees of spiritual healers who have been exposed as fakes continue to offer their faith and 'stick by' the maligned hero, not because of any magnitude of spirit themselves but because of the insupportable psychological consequences of accepting they had been duped.

Festinger showed the power of cognitive dissonance at work in another interesting way. He and an associate asked students to help in an extremely boring, repetitive manual task as part of an experiment. Afterwards, all the students were asked to tell, individually, another student who was also to participate in the same experiment that the task was rather interesting. To motivate them to tell this lie, some of the first team were offered one dollar, others twenty dollars. The first team were later asked to give their reactions to the task they had had to complete. Those paid twenty dollars to say it was interesting to another student admitted they found it boring. Those paid only one dollar tended to say that the task was quite interesting really and more meaningful than they had imagined. What was happening was that both sets of students had had to justify to themselves the telling of the lie. Those who had been paid a considerable amount of money needed only to say, ' I did it for the money'. But those who received a pittance couldn't convince themselves that that was the reason for their lie. So they had to convince themselves that they hadn't really lied at all and that, really, there was something interesting about the task they had to do.

On the same basis, though probably without knowing why, parents often find mild rebukes more effective in stopping disruptive behaviour in children than heavier threats. If a child is threatened with death and destruction if he crayons on the curtains, he may stop for the moment. He will think, 'I only stopped because I was forced to. But I still want to do it.' If he is gently turned to some other activity, he is more likely to justify his change of activity by saying to himself, 'Well, I didn't want to crayon on the curtains anyway, really.'

An amusing experiment, first carried out by Smith and then replicated, with modifications, by Zimbardo, showed that cognitive dissonance can make people start to like eating grasshoppers. Supposedly as an experiment in widening the range of menu in a military college, people were asked to try eating fried grasshoppers, an idea that no one found appealing. When a pleasant man made the request, stressing the voluntariness of its nature, numerous people complied but most still disliked grasshoppers afterwards. When an obnoxious man made the request, earning the dislike of the participants by the rude manner in which he treated his assistant, far more of those who ate claimed to like grasshoppers afterwards. The researchers explained this by cognitive dissonance theory. When the experimenter was a nice guy, the participants could justify their opting to eat something unpleasant by telling themselves they did it because the man was nice enough and they wanted to help him. When the man was not in the least bit likeable, how could they justify eating a food that they weren't even being forced to eat? Only by coming to find that the food itself was quite palatable really, therefore justifying their decision to give it a try.

Ellot Aronson has said: 'Dissonance theory does not rest upon the assumption that man is a *rational* animal; rather, it suggests that man is a rational*ising* animal – that he attempts to appear rational, both to others and to himself.' (*Theories of Cognitive Consistency.*) This need can considerably colour his attitudes.

An experiment by Aronson himself shows how effort invested in an activity can alter perceptions of the activity's worth, all in line with dissonance theory. A group discussion on the psychology of sex was announced. Girls who wanted to join it were divided into three groups. One group was just given permission to join. The other two groups were given some sort of test to see if they were suitable. In one case the 'initiation' was mild. In the other case it was strong, the girls being required to recite swear words in front of a male experimenter. Afterwards all the girls were played a tape, supposedly of a similar psychology of sex discussion that had been held before. The tape was deliberately made extremely boring. Only the women who had suffered the severe initiation process said that they found the discussion interesting. Aronson concludes that the effort put in to joining the group could only be reconciled with achieving something that made it all worth it. Therefore, it would have been impossible for the women who had been made embarrassed to perceive the discussion as boring and to face the fact that they had invested considerable energy in nothing.

Aronson himself admits that there could be other explanations for the girls' behaviour. Perhaps the very reciting of swear words excited the girls and made them anticipate pleasure. Or, if the initiation had embarrassed them, perhaps the discovery that the discussion was in fact banal and not in the least threatening was such a relief that it coloured their judgement of the content. But the outcome is still all too obviously the same: defence of something worthless.

On the same principle of effort made requiring reward , Zimbardo, Brehm and Cohen have found that a speaker who has low credibility can often sway an audience over to his side more easily than a speaker with all the right credentials and reputation, if the people in the audience have had to make an effort to get to hear him. To travel a long distance and then to disagree with an expert is not tension-inducing because the expert is usually considered to be worth hearing. But to go out of one's way to hear someone who has no standing and talks nonsense is more difficult to reconcile with one's own intelligence. Therefore it may be easier to resolve the conflict aroused and the questioning of one's integrity by finding something to agree with the man about.

What is dissonant for one may not be dissonant for another. If a person with a strong self-image feels his marriage isn't working, he may be inclined to stick with it like a leech, to justify his belief in his own judgement of people and the effort he has already made to make the relationship work. 'I can't let go now. It will make the last six years seem worthless.' The person who has a low self-image and who always expects to have everything go wrong will not experience the tension of dissonance in the same situation: 'Just my luck. Nothing ever works out for me.' The bad relationship confirms what he thinks of himself instead of threatening it.

The effects of resolving cognitive dissonance can be far more extensive and harmful than simple self deception. Henry Dicks describes an account of how Nazi thinking took hold, which illustrates the point. From *Licensed Mass Murder* :

'Frau von Baeyer-Katte has skilfully depicted the process of regression towards the acceptance of Nazi group norms

or ethos in various social contexts after the Party came to
power. At mass level there were the constant uniformed
triumphal marches, day-long singing of the Party's "Horst-
Wessel" song, in short the build-up of a "we" feeling
from which no patriotic "decent" person could stand
aside. One had to cheer too. It now became easier to
succumb to the subtly introduced blackmail of Party
pressure through the appearance in offices, industrial
plants, etc., of uniformed or at least openly Nazi "be-
lievers". In the climate of Germany of those days, such
people easily became paranoidally regarded and feared as
planted secret informers. Thus conformity – always a
strong social motive – by colluding with those early
elements of terror, in the shape of "authentic" representatives of the new and required group ethos, replaced
individual rational criticism and moral judgements.
People had to vie with one another in public to mouth the
right sentiments . . . At first a person with an averagely
humane conscience would condemn himself for this lack
of moral courage and self-betrayal. This became too
intolerable – so the second stage was a denial: surely there
had to be *some* truth in what Nazi beliefs he had to assent
to in his group?'

Toch, in *The Social Psychology of Social Movements*,
evocatively describes the dilemma of cognitive dissonance,
without using the word, when he comments on an extremely
personal rude letter sent to an editor of a paper from the
follower of some leader that the editor had written unflatter-
ingly about in print. Commenting on the letter, Toch says,
'The latent message in this communication is something in
the order of "your negative characterisation of one of the
leaders of my movement hurts me deeply because I had come
to rely on this person (and others like him) for security and
support. If what you said were true, I would be in a serious
predicament. I am therefore constrained to regard you as a
very evil person."'
Toch illustrates here not only the nature of the resolution

of dissonance at work but the power to strengthen belief that an attack on that belief can have – as mentioned in Kiesler's work.

Philip Zimbardo, in *Influencing Attitudes and Changing Behaviour*, mentions the role that cognitive dissonance seems to play in the specific case of conversion to the beliefs of the Moonies. He points out that people are invited, not forced, to come on a week-end retreat to hear about the philosophies of Reverend Moon. He suggests that a person who doesn't believe in the philosophies but sees himself behaving like others who do, while uncoerced to do so, will have to reduce the dissonance created by convincing himself he *does* believe in Reverend Moon.

One way to reduce dissonance is to seek social support for one's own position. By finding other people who hold the same views, one can justify one's own holding of them. In the case of cults, says Zimbardo, where old life-styles are abandoned for new, it is necessary to draw as many people as possible into the new life-style so that the ever increasing social support for the decision to join confirms its obvious 'rightness'. (The same sort of thing happened, as we saw, with Mrs Keech's followers, who actively sought converts after they had had to face the dilemma of carrying on believing in Mrs Keech or else acknowledging their own gullibility.)

Dissonance theory may help to explain why some people, when they are converted to a belief, hold on to it longer than others. Hoffman ran an experiment to test the role of conformity needs in the persistence of a conversion. He subjected a number of students to pressure to change their attitudes on a particular topic. Two weeks later, he tested them to see how many still held the new view and how many had reverted to the old. He found that those who had a high need to conform had far lower persistent 'conversion' scores than those who had personalities less prone to conforming. The author says, 'Suggestive is the finding that the longer one resists altering his position under pressure conditions, the longer he retains the altered position in the post-pressure condition.' It might also be said that the longer one resists changing his position, the more need he has to square his change of position with himself, by believing it all the more wholeheartedly.

. Sargant notes the same effect, although he attributes a different reason. He says, in *Battle for the Mind* :

> 'The amount of consolidation needed to fix new patterns of thought and behaviour must depend on the particular type of nervous system as well as on the methods employed. Some persons seem to absorb new doctrines much more readily than others, but the slower or more obstinate types can be trusted to grasp them more securely, once accepted.'

Philip Zimbardo, in an article on cognitive dissonance and the control of human motivation, makes an important observation on the nature of responsibility-taking:

> 'When subjects perceive that they must make an important decision and that they have a choice in committing themselves to one of the possible alternatives, they must then assume responsibility for that decision. This process is one of the few behavioural events which makes them (and us) uniquely human.
>
> 'As the justifications (be they hedonistic, mystical or rational) for making a given decision increase, the decision becomes more "externalised"; the individual can point to circumstances which compel a given course of action, limit his choice and reduce the risks attendant upon personal responsibility. In short, extrinsic justification minimises the necessity for intrinsic justification – for psychological re-evaluation of the alternatives, for changing one's values, attitudes or motives.
>
> 'It appears, from observations of our subjects' behaviour in these experiments and also from less controlled observations, that most people try to avoid making decisions or accepting responsibility and situations of free choice.'

It is an interesting paradox that most people treasure the concept of free choice, verbally defend it or actively pretend to assume it, as in the case of the soldiers who marched to the bathroom, yet, in reality, do all to avoid it. Zimbardo believes that an illusion of personal invulnerability effectively works against the taking of control of one's own life – and works *for* any agents who would take control of it for you. Such beliefs as, 'others could be made to do that but not me' and 'others could be swayed by speeches but not me' are dangerous because they set us apart from other people who *are* like ourselves and therefore prevent us from learning from their experience what may be valuable for ourselves.

Zimbardo compounds the point in his introduction to *Influencing Attitudes and Changing Behaviour* :

> 'Be forewarned that in this text we are actively attempting to reshape your thinking about this sense of invulnerability. We believe you can be more often master of your own destiny if you learn to identify potential or existing sources of influence. We know we have set a difficult task for ourselves because research tells us that you are likely to ignore information about how the majority of people in a given situation react and to favour information about the isolated cases that fit your preconceptions or personal preferences.'

It is no doubt very true that we never consider that we are the majority that wouldn't rush to the help of someone in an emergency or that would give electric shocks to an innocent party. We instead absolve ourselves from the collective responsibility of such findings by saying, '*I* wouldn't have done that.' And that is yet another example of cognitive dissonance at work.

The placebo effect

The power of belief is a remarkable force for changing the expected or normal course of events, often enough unknown to the believer. Many are the tales told of members of primitive tribes who, once told by a witch doctor that they will die or once cursed by an enemy, proceed to die when there is no physiological indication of imminent death. Similarly, belief in the spiritual healing process can effect a cure for even intransigent diseases. While it is not the aim here to debate the contribution of the healer himself, it is worth quoting one case in which a doctor told three extremely ill women that a remarkable faith healer could cure them by absent healing. He built up their expectations and told them the time of the day that the healer would set to work. No healer set to work. But, after the appointed time, all three women showed dramatic improvement. One, who had never recovered from a major operation on the stomach and had dwindled to nothing in weight, made a permanent recovery. Another had suffered chronic inflammation of the gall bladder. Her symptoms disappeared for years. The third, who was dying painfully of cancer lost all her symptoms and was trouble-free until her death.

Such belief has its uses in traditional medicine. Biologically inert substances, properly called placebos, colloquially known as sugar pills, can effect cures as efficiently as pharmacologically active drugs.

Placebos are commonly used in drug-testing. One set of patients are given a real drug, the other an inactive substance. If the patients who take the real drug improve and the patients who take the placebo don't, the improvement can safely be attributed to the drug and not to other factors. However, here human nature comes in to confuse the issue. Many people, known as placebo reactors, also demonstrate the desired improvements without the benefit of any chemical agents.

The expectation that a sugar pill will induce the effects a doctor claims for it can lead to some bizarre physiological contradictions. For instance, a man suffering from severe nausea was given a drug that would normally induce vomiting. However, he was told that it would *cure* his vomiting and it did.

Some people who are given placebos even claim to suffer side effects as well as improvements. And some people, given red, yellow and blue placebos to try as a headache cure, reported back that only one colour pill worked. The most popularly effective placebo was the red one!

People who are placebo reactors have been found, in research, to be more neurotic, suggestible and submissive than non-reactors.

In *Persuasion and Healing*, Jerome Frank says: 'Since a placebo is inert, its beneficial effects must lie in its symbolic power. The most likely supposition is that it gains its potency through being a tangible symbol of the physician's role as a healer.' Once again we need to believe that someone is 'in charge'.

Believing in a healer may well serve to reduce anxiety about one's condition and, as the conditions that respond best to placebos are those where bodily pain may be aggravated by anxiety and tension, this would tend to imply that placebo power is the power to allay the kind of stress symptoms which may prevent the body's own healing process from getting to work. It makes all the more sense when one considers that more and more diseases are now seen as stress-induced in the first place.

Frank mentions the placebo treatment of warts: the warts are painted with a bright dye and the patient is told that when the dye wears off the warts will be gone. Here the success rate, which is high, may be attributed to the physiological effects of the power of belief. The emotional reaction to the placebo treatment, with the expectation of cure, causes a change in the physiology of the skin, which creates an environment no longer conducive to the virus that causes warts.

Electro-convulsive therapy for the treatment of depression – the vital ingredient of which, according to Sargant, is the current through the brain that induces a convulsion – can work just as effectively without any current at all. An English doctor discovered that his ECT machine hadn't been functioning for two years, although it was thought to be working and consequently used every day. The patients had 'improved' in accordance with expectation, both their own and the doctor's, yet nothing had happened at all. This finding, that the ambience of the ECT treatment might be the potent factor, not the shock, was later confirmed in a controlled trial.

Placebo treatment is mentioned here to demonstrate the very real effects of suggestibility, expectation and belief, which can be manifested in many different sorts of circumstances, not just medical. It was earlier mentioned that a belief in the power of hypnosis was sufficient to make it work. One's own mental state can therefore significantly affect the outcome of events and impose its own order on an environment. While this, in some circumstances, may be a strength to be capitalised on, it may also be a vulnerability that others can take advantage of. Again, only by questioning assumptions can one isolate causes from effects.

The weapons effect

In *The Writing on the Wall*, McCarthy says in defence of her belief that it is possible to behave well whatever the circumstances:

'Nobody by possession of a weapon can force a man to kill anybody; that is his own decision. If somebody points a gun at you and says "Kill your friend or I will kill you", he is *tempting* you to kill your friend. That is all.'

Or maybe it is not all. Some American psychologists have found that the 'weapons effect' works in far more insidious ways to influence behaviour. Merely the sight of a gun can alter reactions, and not just on the part of the person wielding the weapon.

Recently Turner, Simons and associates carried out a couple of intriguing experiments to prove the point. On two occasions they invited students at a college carnival to throw sponges at a clown. The first time, a rifle was left in a conspicuous position in front of the booth where the clown was standing. On the second occasion, there was no rifle on view. Both times, the clown hurled insults at some of the sponge throwers to see if his hostile manner made them more aggressive in their throwing. It was found that insults had no effect on the students' behaviour. What did have a marked effect was the innocent – or not so innocent – presence of the rifle. Students who saw the rifle, reacted far more aggressively than the rest, throwing considerably more sponges at the clown.

In a second experiment, the researchers arranged for a truck to stall at a busy junction. On some occasions, the truck displayed a rifle in a gun rack, clearly visible to cars behind. At other times, there was no gun. The researchers found that cars behind honked more, and more persistently, at the stalled truck if it had a rifle in the rack.

Leonard Berkowitz, who carried out the first experiments on the weapons effect more than ten years ago, and whose findings aroused no little controversy, believes that the latest research confirms his early conclusion that 'the finger pulls the trigger but the trigger may also be pulling the finger'.

Berkowitz considers that weapons act as a conditioned stimulus eliciting a conditioned response. Turner offers another but similar explanation, which leans more on information-processing concepts. He holds that guns remind people of occasions when they have seen aggression rewarded, for example, on television where the villain or the hero may use a gun to get his way. It becomes easy therefore to connect guns with the rewards of aggression and, on catching sight of a gun in whatever context, to act more aggressively than normal habits would allow. Needless to say, all the researchers support the case for less violence on television. (*Psychology Today*, June 1981.)

Role-playing

It has already been suggested by various researchers, in the context of conditioning and hypnosis, that participating in the action helps elicit the desired response. Psychologists have shown through controlled experiments that participating in various events, even supposedly as a game, can definitely make an individual's attitude towards that event more positive than before.

In studies, for instance, where students have been asked to improvise arguments for a position that they do not themselves hold, their attitudes towards that position have been shown to be strengthened. Acting out was more effective for inducing attitude change than reading aloud from a script – not only in themselves but in those hearing them. However, the strongest changes came about in the attitudes of those who did the actual role playing.

Trying to identify with another person's point of view is not as effective as acting it out. In an experiment with college students where each had to take a turn in acting a role, then trying to identify with someone else playing a role and, lastly, just watching someone performing a role, as an objective observer, all the students had taken on more of the views of the person they had role-played than those of the person they had tried to identify with or had just listened to. One experimenter, Hovland, commented on the power of improvisation as an attitude changer by saying that it required a person to think up all the arguments and appeals that he thinks would be most convincing to a person like himself – and in so doing, it is himself he persuades. Also, the very act of improvising a role precludes rational weighing up of alternatives. All energy goes into portraying the appeal of the message.

Role playing is much used in therapy, to encourage patients to empathise with the position of important others. For instance, a man who had had a grudge against his mother all his life might come to appreciate her feelings more if he were obliged to act her part in a particular scenario while someone else plays his own. This is a feature of psychodrama. It has also been suggested that trade union and management representatives, at loggerheads because perceptual set (see Chapter 3) prevents them from seeing another point of view, might do well to switch roles in order to open up their perspective.

In encounter groups, a common ploy is to get a person to act out repressed anger by beating a pillow and pretending that the pillow is his wife/mother/father, etc. What starts out as forced artificial attempts at anger soon tends to be overtaken by the real thing, with the person often overcome by the intensity of his angry emotions which emerge full-flow. Role-playing emotion can thus precipitate real emotion. Writing an essay on a given subject can have similar effects to role playing. An individual is required to think up arguments to sustain a position he may not hold and the creative act is sufficient to make those ideas start to gel in his own head.

A recent piece of research indicated that committing something to paper reinforces our belief in it, whatever it is we have written. Three psychologists at Rice University in Houston, Texas, showed students a passage about fire-fighting which either indicated that the successful fire-fighter took risks or else that he played it safe. A third of the students were then asked to write about the relationship between fire-fighting and risk-taking. Then they and another third were told that all the information had been made up. Later all the groups were given a test to see if they still held to the views that the information had suggested. The group that did not know the material had been invented was, as expected, the most swayed by its content. But, of the rest, the students who had had to write about risk-taking and successful fire-fighting were far more strongly entrenched in the belief that it was true than those who had just read it and then been disabused of its credibility. (*Psychology Today*, May 1981, p 17.)

Participation as a tactic for winning people over to one's side has been seen at work in Korea. Prisoners were required to write confessions and autobiographies, the very act of doing which may have firmed up the validity of what they produced. It will be seen again in the context of cults and other political groups, in Chapter 8.

Sensory deprivation

Sensory deprivation experiments, involving the subjects in remaining without stimulation of any kind in lightproof and soundproof rooms, have produced conflicting results about the effects of sensory deprivation on human behaviour. Some people can and do adapt, others experience hallucinations very quickly and lose all sense of time. Which effect will be produced in which person largely depends on the individual's normal needs for external stimulation, the extrovert suffering more than the introvert. However, it has been shown that sensory deprivation slows down brain functioning, impairs intellectual capacities and increases suggestibility. (See *Inside the Black Room*.)

One experiment was carried out by Dr Svedfeld at Princeton University to measure the effect of sensory deprivation on susceptibility to propaganda. His aim was to produce an attitude change favourable to Turkey in people whose attitudes had previously been neutral. Half of Svedfeld's subjects were confined under sensory deprivation conditions for 24 hours. The other half could move about the university building as they pleased. Afterwards all the students heard propaganda favourable to Turkey. The sensory-deprivation students experienced an attitude change in the way intended that was eight times as great as that experienced by the non-confined students.

Professor Jack Vernon of Princeton University carried out a large number of sensory deprivation experiments and, in his book *Inside the Black Room*, suggests a scenario for creating attitude change which incorporates findings from sensory deprivation research, conditioning, cognitive dissonance, dependence, obedience to authority and participation as means of attitude change. This is the scene he proposed.

He notes first that both in the softening-up process preceding brainwashing and in the sensory deprivation condition, a confined person will experience such dreadful monotony and boredom that he will be grateful for absolutely any novelty to distract him. This could be taken advantage of, says Vernon, if the aim is to instil a particular belief in a person. He suggests, for the experiment's sake, that someone who is a strong Protestant, although he doesn't know much about Protestantism, is to be converted to Islam, about which he knows very little either but he is prejudiced enough to hate Muslims. To convert him, says Vernon, the best procedure would be to leave him in sensory deprivation conditions for up to four days, to bring him to the point where he is desperate for stimulus of any kind. Then Vernon would introduce, without any explanation, two switches into the cubicle.

The 'prisoner' would soon find that if he pressed button A, he heard a speech favouring Protestantism. If he pressed button B, he got a speech favouring Islam. But the difference was that button A always produced the same speech on Protestantism whereas button B released an endless variety of speeches on Islam, all delivered by different voices. Desire for novelty would lead the prisoner to start selecting button B over button A.

'We have caused this individual by *his own choice* to listen to our propaganda. If we can get him to listen, we can get him to believe by making our propaganda clever enough,' says Vernon, and it isn't all supposition. An experiment at McGill University in Canada found that subjects did indeed listen more often to varied unfavoured items than the same favoured item when in a condition of having no other choice.

But Vernon carries on. Even if the prisoner does insist on using button A, it still works against him, he says, because repetition can weaken meaning. He recalls the familiar experience of repeating a word over and over and finding that it suddenly becomes strange, as though it is a new word. Its meaning seems to have weakened.

Vernon says, 'It seems reasonable to believe that something similar to this process could happen as a result of a repetition of a slogan' and refers to the Chinese usage, perhaps unwittingly, of this technique in Korea. Prisoners had to write their autobiographies over and over and consequently got very bored: 'The Chinese probably did not realise that it was the monotonous repetition that was weakening some of the soldiers' cherished beliefs; they were only looking for discrepancies in the reports. These were considered to be signs of weak areas and consequently the logical focus of their psychological attack to convert the prisoner to communism.'

Our prisoner, meanwhile, is still listening to the propaganda. Vernon says that now is the time to reward any signs of conversion. So the prisoner is asked questions about Islam over the intercom. If he replies in the desired way, he might get a little light or a new kind of food. Later he might even be allowed to talk to someone in person. Vernon points out that this reward tactic for right responses was certainly commonly used by the Chinese and suggests why they were so often successful: 'These responses are forthcoming from the individual and not forced out of him by pain or punishment, thereby making them more nearly his own beliefs.'

Still acting the role of the propagandist, Vernon pursues his theme even further:

'We now feel that we can devise a system that will enhance the increased suggestibility to an even greater extent. It is possible that the suggestions given by the experimenter will be much more effective if he is established as a figure of authority in the mind of the subject. Suggestibility probably can be increased if the subject is more dependent upon the experimenter *during* the sensory deprivation; for example, if the experimenter gives him his meals, permission to leave the bed to go to the toilet, tells him when he may sleep, interrupts his sleep with occasional tasks, regulates his water supply and in general becomes part of his every activity, at the same time keeping his activities to a minimum.'

Vernon's hypothesis is not outlandish nor particularly difficult to arrange. And it certainly takes advantage of all that is known about attitude influence techniques. From real studies on suggestibility in sensory deprivation conditions, Vernon found that suggestibility in all ways could be increased after two to three days and become four times greater than before. But he also found that it was lost no longer than two days after the experimental conditions were terminated, if gains were not consolidated thereafter.

Why should one become suggestible in such conditions?

Vernon explains that the brainstem reticular formation acts as a way station for all messages coming in and going out of the brain. Normally it inhibits some messages and enhances others, thus dictating which ones get paid conscious attention. Conditions of sensory deprivation probably reduce the amount of information passing through the reticular formation, suggests Vernon: 'If this is the case, then the "importance" of any given sets of neural events may be greatly enhanced. Said more simply, under the conditions of sensory deprivation, the human may be able to content himself with ideas or cognitions that he would otherwise simply dismiss.'

This chapter and the previous three have attempted to highlight the part that conditioned learning, conditioned emotions, unquestioned assumptions and unconscious social behaviour (which produced the 'brainwashing' effect on American POWs in Korea) can also play, individually, to influence ordinary everyday behaviour and decisions. The next chapters investigate whether such processes, singly or in combination, may help to explain how hypnosis works, how dramatic political and religious conversions are experienced and how respected authority figures, such as the police and doctors, can unwittingly direct behaviour in ordinary society.

7 HYPNOSIS

Perhaps because it is not clearly understood how or why a state of consciousness known as hypnosis should exist, the concept tends to arouse strong reactions, ranging from fear and curiosity to disbelief, in very many people. What exactly is hypnosis? Can it be induced without one's knowledge? Can it force one to act against one's will? Is it a high-powered mind manipulating technique? And if it exists as a state of consciousness, why can't everyone be hypnotised? Or can they?

Certainly the power potential of the hypnotiser encouraged the CIA to spend some years investigating hypnosis as a means for programming assassins or for sending top secret messages that would be forgotten the instant after delivery. The accounts of their activities featured in various books, such as *The Mind Manipulators* by Scheflin and Opton, *Operation Mind Control* by Walter Bowart and *The Search for 'The Manchurian Candidate'* by John Marks, all seem to indicate that they didn't get very far. However, many psychological researchers have spent years studying the hypnotic state and have come up with various, conflicting theories as to why it works and whom it works with.

Ernest Hilgard and colleagues at Stanford University some years ago developed a hypnotic susceptibility scale which set certain criteria for assessing people's responses under hypnosis to commands such as, 'You cannot separate your hands' or 'You cannot say your name'. He concluded that between five and ten per cent of the population is highly susceptible to hypnosis and the same number are completely resistant against it, with the rest of the population falling somewhere in between. Thus, according to Hilgard's findings, most people can be hypnotised but some more easily than others.

This conclusion has been broadly accepted for many years. But recently another American psychologist has started to question it. Professor Joe Barber of the University of California in Los Angeles Medical School now claims that *everyone* is susceptible to hypnosis and that people who appear to be resistant are not resistant to hypnosis itself but to the way it is traditionally induced. Some individuals, he claims, are simply hostile to the monotonous lugubrious deliberately slow tones adopted by hypnotists to induce trance and also react defensively against direct commands such as 'You *will* feel sleepy' or 'Your eyes *will* close'. Whereas, according to Barber, if the hypnotist adopts a conversational, non-authoritarian approach, suggesting in a normal voice gentle ideas such as, 'I wonder if you find it surprising that your eyes can start to feel heavy so quickly', there can be a one hundred per cent success rate.

Professor Barber has tried this method himself with numerous subjects. In one experiment, he attempted to hypnotise 27 people and then subjected them all to extremely painful electrical stimulation of the nerve fibres in the teeth. Not one of the 27 felt the slightest pain. Accordingly, Professor Barber believes that hypnosis, correctly induced, has an as yet not fully tapped contribution to make in the field of pain control.

Because of a misconception as to what the state of hypnosis is, many people presume they are not being successfully hypnotised because they are not asleep. In fact hypnosis is a conscious state, identified physiologically as producing the same brainwave pattern as that which occurs when people are in a relaxed state – alpha rhythms. (Beta rhythms are associated with normal, waking activity, theta rhythms appear when a person is slipping from wakefulness into sleep and delta rhythms occur during deep sleep.) The trance, as it is commonly called, is not a single specific definable state but more accurately covers anything from relatively light to very deep relaxation. Professor Barber, for instance, has said that anyone who is absorbed in what someone else is saying is in a light state of trance.

The state of hypnosis is commonly defined as a state of heightened suggestibility, thus providing the stage hypnotist with the opportunity to suggest to a subject that he carry out certain acts designed to amuse the rest of the audience, or the hypnotherapist with the chance to instil confidence in a patient, or, because defences are down, to draw out the buried details of a troubled past. But certain researchers believe that a state of suggestibility is just a normal waking condition, more notable in some people than others, and that there is no need to designate it as a special state called hypnosis. A vocal supporter of this view is Dr Theodore Barber, an expert hypnotist and respected hypnosis researcher of over twenty years, and director of special projects at the Cushing Hospital in Framingham, Massachussetts.

The main thrust of Barber's argument is that the kind of people who can perform the most interesting mental feats under hypnosis can in fact perform them without the aid of any induced hypnosis at all. On the basis of his research he claims that between three to four per cent of the female population at least can hallucinate at will, touch apparitions and have out of the body experiences and that most of such women are leading normal, active lives, unaware that their powers are anything special. Such abilities are found, says Barber, not in accordance with certain levels of education or types of personality or emotional stability but in women who share one basic trait: a tendency to have fantasised from an early age and to continue an intense fantasy life as adults.

Barber made this discovery almost by accident. He had set out to research what characteristics, if any, so-called 'somnambules' had in common. Somnambule is the name given to people who are so susceptible to hypnosis that they can be induced to experience specific sensations, such as heat or cold, to smell or taste to order, to suffer amnesia for any event or to regress to 'past lives', and reliably to carry out post-hypnotic suggestions.

Barber gave hypnotisability tests to over 900 people and found nineteen women, aged from twenty-one to forty-seven, who were clearly somnambules. (Since he reported his research, Barber has carried out even wider testing and now has over 30 somnambules, some of them men.) When Barber later interviewed and tested his nineteen highly hypnotisable women in depth, he made the discovery that they were so easy to hypnotise purely because they could also hypnotise themselves. They didn't need a hypnotist. 'There was nothing they could be made to do under hypnosis that they couldn't do of their own free will,' he said.

It appeared that,as children, all the women had lived for the most part in a fantasy world of their own, very often shared by imaginary playmates that were real enough to touch, see and hear. As adults, none of the group spent less than 50 per cent of their time in fantasy and the majority estimated that a full nine-tenths of their time was spent in an imaginary world that co-existed with their ordinary one. For instance, they could fantasise at work without actually losing concentration for the task at hand.

It was common for a word or a sight or sound to trigger their imagination and almost literally transport them to a place that the sensation conjured up. For instance, the name of a country was enough to set in motion an intense living fantasy of foreign parts. One subject, during an interview about her abilities, enthused: 'Fantasy is being anything you can be, could be or are. It's possibilities made possible. It's soaring, thrilling, living! Who's to say what's happening right now is reality?'

Most intriguing and convincing for Barber was the fact that the fantasies didn't stay firmly entrenched in the nebulous realm of the mind. They had physical manifestations, which were often measurable: most could reach orgasm by sexual fantasy alone; eleven out of fourteen who were asked admitted to having had at least one phantom pregnancy, with all the associated symptoms of lack of periods, breast changes, cravings and the feeling of foetal movements inside; they could experience heat or cold, just by imagining it.

Experiences of telepathy, precognition and the unintentional or intentional summoning up of lifelike apparitions were all part of daily life to the somnambule women. They could also remember their childhood in amazingly vivid detail. Few of the women, it transpired from the interviews, realised that all other people did *not* regularly have similar experiences. The women came from all walks of life and most were emotionally stable, usually living within a long-established couple relationship. (All these findings were reported at the annual meeting of the American Association for the Study of Mental Imagery, in Minneapolis, June 20, 1980.)

Various psychiatrists have, independently, over the last few years come to the conclusion that unwitting abuse of self-hypnosis may lead to the emergence of multiple personalities and exotic-type phobias. Dr Eugene Bliss, a Utah psychiatrist who studied fourteen cases of multiple personality, found that the patients all created their first 'personality' early in childhood, to combat loneliness or insecurity, could all remember their childhood in detail and were all easily hypnotised. They could also distort their own higher brain functions, so as to reduce or enhance sensations or block out memories.

A patient whom Dr Morton Schatzman has written about in *The Story of Ruth* came into treatment because she kept seeing apparitions of her father. Taught in treatment to 'create' such apparitions for herself, she could summon apparitions of anyone at will. In one scientific investigation of her abilities it was discovered that, if she summoned an apparition of her daughter to sit on her lap in such a way that the apparition's head blocked out the light from a lamp, Ruth's brain actually registered no response to the light from that lamp.

Psychiatrists Frankel and Orne, in an experiment on hypnosis as an effective cure for smokers and phobias, found that no phobic patient was unresponsive to being hypnotised (whereas many smokers were) and that the more phobias they had, the more susceptible to hypnosis they became. The psychiatrists wrote in *Archives of General Psychiatry*:

'These findings suggest that individuals who develop phobic symptoms must have the capability of manifesting . . . the kind of mental process where images and fantasies can become sufficiently vivid and real to be confused with the world outside.'

The ramifications of such findings are wider than just the possible discovery of what lies behind hypnotic suggestibility. However, even in more traditional hypnosis research, it has long been asserted that imagination plays a part in creating suggestibility. Hilgard, from assessment of the personality types most associated with somnambulism, claims that early childhood experience plays a strong part and stresses imaginative experiences, interests such as music and reading which require a strong personal involvement in the activity itself and also excessive parental punishment, which could lead a child not only to become obedient and reliant (an ingredient in responsiveness to hypnosis) but to withdraw into fantasy to escape.

Sarbin and Lim also linked imagination to susceptibility. By judging people's abilities to play-act given roles, the researchers were able to establish that those who were most easily hypnotised were also those who could most easily assume a part while play-acting roles.

Role playing itself is seen as the main constituent of hypnosis by researchers such as Martin Orne, another leading investigator in the field. Orne, professor of psychiatry at the University of Pennsylvania, carried out a now celebrated experiment to prove his point. He claimed that the so-called state of hypnosis was created by the combined wish of the hypnotist and subject to fulfil each other's expectations. Cues as to what is expected are given by the hypnotist and picked up on by the subject. In his experiment, Orne gave a lecture to two different groups of students about hypnosis. One group was told that the state of hypnosis was signalled by the subject's inability to move whichever was his dominant hand and a 'demonstration' of this fact was arranged. The other group was not told any such thing.

Later Orne hypnotised volunteers from both groups. Those who had seen the immobile-hand demonstration all found they couldn't move their dominant hand when hypnotised. Those that had not seen the demonstration could move both hands quite freely under hypnosis.

Orne concluded that people act under hypnosis as they think they are supposed to act. If they are keen to please, they can be hypnotised to order. More will be said about Orne's theory that a subject must not only want to be hypnotised but have a positive relationship with the hypnotist when hypnosis against will is discussed.

Hilgard took issue with Orne's findings and carried out an experiment designed to show that more than role playing is involved in hypnotism. He had twenty students thrust their arms, up to the elbow, in ice cold water so that he could record their normal pain endurance. Then he hypnotised ten and told them that they would feel no pain when he asked them to immerse their arms a second time. The other ten were told the same thing but while *not* under hypnosis. In the event, Hilgard found that the suggestion alone that they would not feel pain was sufficient to increase tolerance to the cold but that it fell far short of the tolerance exhibited by those who had been assured while under hypnosis that they would not feel pain. Hilgard concluded that there was evidence, therefore, that people could get pain relief by hypnotic suggestion; they were not merely keeping their sufferings to themselves in order to please the hypnotist.

A study of hypnosis and pain was carried out at the Wright-Patterson Aerospace Medical Laboratories in Ohio, according to Vance Packard in *The People Shapers*. The goal was to establish how aerospace pilots could best be kept alert during emergencies where they might be suffering debilitating extremes of heat and cold. Hypnotised students were put in special hot compartments and told to keep working on a specified task. They learned to carry on functioning efficiently in temperatures of 140°. One student said that he had actually felt cool; he had been imagining he was a lifeguard at a swimming pool. Barber might construe that the student was achieving his end by his ability to fantasise, rather than by the power of hypnosis.

Yet another theory as to why hypnosis works has been ardently proposed and defended by the American psychologist Andrew Salter. He believes that hypnosis is simply a form of conditioning.

Pavlov, during his work on conditioning, first posited that suggestibility was the most simple type of conditioned reflex in man because speech could serve as a conditioned stimulus. Thus, just as dogs might salivate to a bell, if they associated it with food, so humans might salivate on hearing the words, 'roast chicken' or 'peppered steak', because these words had become associated with the real thing. Salter, an arch opponent of Barber's theories, takes this idea on to explain hypnosis and various other 'inexplicable' phenomena such as hallucination. In his own words from his book, *Conditioned Reflex Therapy*:

'What does a spectator see when a good subject is hypnotised? The hypnotist (unfortunate word) says in a soporific voice, "Your eyes are so *heavy* . . ."

'Does it not seem plausible that the word "heavy" in good subjects was associated with heavy feelings and that the repetition of the word "heavy" by the hypnotist acted as the bell of past associations of *actual* heavy feelings? In a sense, then, hypnotists are persons who ring standard bells and find some dogs who were trained to salivate to them, in this instance, people who feel heavy and tired. "Behold," they say, "here is a good subject." How meaningless.

'How easy to understand are the shivers that appropriate hypnotic "suggestion" of ice and snow produces in a good subject. He processes verbally conditioned bells waiting to be rung.'

He goes on to explain pain relief and the experience of

hallucination by similar means. As regards pain, he draws attention to the fact that it is common to discover with surprise bruises on one's body that indicated some severe blow but one which wasn't registered at the time, presumably because attention was elsewhere. Therefore, when hypnotised not to feel pain, what is happening is that the hypnotist's statements about the subject's inability to feel any forthcoming pain trigger '*established* reaction systems of anaesthesia'.

He refers to an experiment, carried out by Ellson and reported in the *Journal of Experimental Psychiatry*, where subjects were shown a light and heard a tone simultaneously. Thirty-two out of 42 subjects later reported hearing the tone when only the light was shown. Salter concludes:

> 'This means that eighty per cent of the subjects in this experiment could not tell the difference between a *bona fide* sound and their own hallucinations. When we realise that sights and sounds can be conditioned and that the bells that conjure them up may be set off internally, we can understand why Luther threw an inkpot at the devil and from whence came the voices heard by Joan of Arc and Mohammed, to say nothing of the ghosts sincerely reported by more mundane persons.
>
> 'There can be no question that hallucinations in hypnosis and the sensory miracles associated with various saints are essentially genuine and explicable phenomena of conditioning. Hunger, fatigue, and excitement, all of which reduce inhibition, would facilitate hallucinatory experiences.'

Salter goes on to make his perhaps most controversial claim: that, if hypnosis is, as he believes, purely an aspect of conditioning, then it should be perfectly possible to train people to carry out anti-social acts or harm themselves or others. In short, suggestion need not fit in with moral code and therefore, under hypnosis, a person could be led to undertake to commit a crime:

> 'Hypnosis is not the production of a state. It is the eliciting

of one. But if the reflex patterns in hypnotic subjects are there at the start, and such seems to be the case, we are forced to entertain the curious conclusion that suggestion does not implant anything. But this is not so. Hypnosis takes advantage of something already there in order to plant something new.'

Salter points out that, just as intelligent people are most easy to condition, so are they easiest to hypnotise. Perry London, in *Behaviour Control*, arrives by a different route at the conclusion that hypnosis and conditioning, if not identical, are indeed linked. He participated in a study which demonstrated that the more susceptible people are to hypnosis, the higher their general level of brainwave activity. He goes on to say:

'The "mental" character of hypnosis also makes it appear to be the opposite of conditioning, which is an evolutionary spin-off of the spinal reflex, a system of parleying primitive muscle and gland action into fancy behaviour. Hypnosis begins its effects in the higher brain centers where it is induced by means of speech; it starts at the mind and works downward. In that sense, desensitisation and implosive therapy (flooding) are both akin to hypnosis: they aim at the mind directly, primarily by verbal means and they use the images conjured by the therapist as catalysts for manipulating the emotional responses of the patient. But they are also conditioning methods, producing the same effects by the same means on human beings as on cats and rats. They thus represent a bridge between hypnosis and conditioning which may be more closely related processes, physiologically, than is now known.'

To return to the contentious topic raised a moment ago: hypnosis against will. Andrew Salter is not the only one to believe in hypnosis as a method of manipulating behaviour in a way that goes against the grain. George Estabrooks, who also equated hypnosis with conditioning, has waxed lyrical in books such as *Hypnotism* and *The Future of the Human Mind* about fantasised possibilities of programming assassins. And there are those prepared to say that Sirhan Beshara Sirhan, the killer of Robert Kennedy, indeed was one. Walter Bowart quotes two experts in *Operation Mind Control*. Dr John W. Heisse Jr, president of the International Society of Stress Analysis, studied Sirhan's psychiatric charts and interviews and his performance on the PSE (Psychological Stress Evaluator).

He concluded: 'Sirhan kept repeating certain phrases. This clearly revealed he had been programmed to put himself into a trance. This is something he couldn't have learned by himself. Someone had to show him and teach him how. I believe Sirhan was brainwashed under hypnosis by the constant repetition of words like, "You are nobody, you're nothing, the American dream is gone" until he actually believed them. At that stage, someone implanted an idea, "kill Robert F. Kennedy", and under hypnosis the brainwashed Sirhan accepted it.'

Similarly, Dr Herbert Spiegel, a medical expert on hypnosis: 'It's very possible to distort and change somebody's mind through a number of hypnotic sessions. It can be described as brainwashing because the mind is cleared of its old emotions and values which are replaced by implanting other suggestions. . . . This technique was probably used with Sirhan. From my own research, I think Sirhan was subjected to hypnotic treatment.'

Whatever the truth of that, years earlier Morse Allen, head of CIA's project BLUEBIRD, established in 1950 to investigate agents and defectors, using mind control means, had initiated his own experiments into the possibility of hypnotising people against their will and programming assassins. The experiments were documented in a long series of memos to which John Marks gained access and referred to in *The Search for the 'Manchurian Candidate'*. Having undertaken a four day course in hypnotism with a stage hypnotist, Allen set about hypnotising CIA secretaries and getting them to steal secret files and pass them on to people whom they supposed were total strangers, to steal from each other and to start fires. In February 1954 he simulated the creation of a programmed assassin. He hypnotised one secretary and told her to fall asleep and stay asleep. Then he hypnotised another secretary and told her that, if she couldn't wake her friend, she would become so enraged that she would kill her. He then left an unloaded pistol near at hand. Even though the girl had professed herself terrified of firearms, she did 'shoot' her friend. Afterwards she blocked out the event from her mind and swore that she could never be made to kill anyone.

Allen didn't run away with the idea, from this success, that he had succeeded in finding the means to programme assassins. He felt far from sure that he could repeat his success in any less experimental setting. To quote Marks: 'All he felt he had proved was that an impressionable young volunteer would accept a command from a legitimate authority figure to take an action she may have sensed would not end in tragedy. She presumably trusted the CIA enough as an institution and Morse Allen as an individual to believe he would not let her do anything wrong. The experimental setting, in effect, legitimated her behaviour and prevented it from being truly anti-social.'

An experiment of Martin Orne's serves to confirm Allen's reservations. Hypnotised subjects were asked to throw a beaker of acid into the face of one of the people present in the laboratory during the experiment. The subjects had seen the hypnotist drop a coin in the beaker and had seen it dissolve, yet they did fling the acid at the person. (The set up of the experiment prevented actual harm from being done.) It would be easy to conclude that hypnosis is indeed powerful enough to force people to act against ordinary judgement. However, Orne showed that hypnosis was not the essential ingredient in the act. He carried out the same experiment with non-hypnotised subjects – and they acted in exactly the same way. What was proved was not that hypnosis can cloud judgement but that entrenched ideas of obedience to authority can do so. (See Milgram's experiment with electric shocks in Chapter 2.) The subjects had accepted the *role* of subjects, and all the compliance with experimenters' authority that that implied.

In an article published in *The Manipulation of Human Behaviour*, edited by Biderman and Zimmer, Orne discusses his view that hypnosis cannot induce people to act against their will because the hypnotic state is dependent on the positive relationship between the hypnotist and subject and their wish to cooperate. All the studies that he had investigated of people being hypnotised unawares (e.g. when a therapist gets a patient to relax but is really using hypnotism without using the word) or of being hypnotised against their will seemed to depend for their success on the relationship that had been established between the subject and hypnotist. The only three cases of real criminal acts involving hypnotism that Orne said he knew of (and where the people concerned claimed they didn't know they had been hypnotised to commit those acts) all involved 'an intense emotional relationship between hypnotist and patient'. All cases of attempts to induce antisocial acts by hypnotism where the hypnotist and subject had never met previously failed.

Meerloo has another explanation for why anti-social acts committed as a result of hypnosis only *seem* to be contrary to will:

'There are many anti-social desires lying hidden in all people. The hypnotic technique, if cleverly enough applied, can bring them to the surface and cause them to be acted out in life.'

Hypnotherapists tend to claim that it is impossible to force the unconscious to yield up information it is not ready to give (the aim of therapy, of course, being to reach what is buried in the unconscious mind and which may be the cause of some manifested problem, such as a phobia or anxiety panics). It is, however, known and accepted that a hypnotist, by distorting a person's reality, can make him act contrary to his normal moral or social codes. For instance, it would be possible to induce a person to walk about naked in a room filled with people if that person had first been made to believe the room was empty.

Field and Dworkin published an article in the *Journal of Psychiatry* showing that it is by no means an easy thing to induce subjects, by hypnosis, to reveal what they do not wish to reveal during interrogation. The subjects were given information that they were told not to disclose under any circumstances during the experiment. Then they were hypnotised and told, for instance, that their guilt at lying would make them tell the truth or that they would reveal themselves by making a strong involuntary movement after a lie which the lie detector would detect. The test required the subjects to think of a number and then try to prevent the experimenter from guessing it as he counted down.

Only six out of 26 subjects revealed their number, either through 'guilt' or through an involuntary jerk as it was spoken. Four times the revelation was forced by the lie detector test, only twice did the guilt method extract the correct number.

The authors concluded that only very highly hypnotisable subjects could be made to crack under hypnosis, although it could be objected that there would be considerably less emotional investment in keeping an arbitrary number concealed than some more personal piece of information.

Finally, it is worth reiterating, as Biderman does, that there is yet another factor that could be crucial to the success of hypnotic techniques, regardless of whether role-playing, conditioning, imagination or rapport is involved. If people *believe* that when they are hypnotised, they are not in control of their actions, they may well be the more ready to abdicate responsibility for what they do. So, if, as in Korea, a prisoner felt he was no longer master of his fate, he might be induced under hypnosis to reveal information he would never normally give because, in that situation, he could feel justified in attaching no blame to his actions. More has been said of the power of belief in Chapter 6.

Suffice it to say here that hypnosis, far from being some

simple, easy to define and universally agreed-on state, seems likely to be linked with any one of a number of disparate personality and behaviour traits, just as seems to be the case with brainwashing. It will be seen that those very traits play a significant part in other types of attitude influence and the so-called brainwashing process itself.

8 SUDDEN CONVERSION

One is rarely accused of being brainwashed if, after a lifetime of agnosticism or political inertia, one suddenly embraces Catholicism or joins the Labour party. However, if one's new allegiance involves contravention of all conventional morality or diversion from societal norms, it is questioned whether it could have been adopted of free will. So one may choose to become a Catholic but the Moonies choose you. That the latter 'choice' merely represents a more vivid confluence of the kinds of psychological forces so far discussed is rarely considered. But the conversion process can be broken down into its component parts in much the same way that the experts dissected the 'brainwashing' experience in Korea. In the course of this chapter, three recent celebrated cases of conversion, all of which led to court cases where the word 'brainwashing' was bandied freely by either the prosecution or the defence, will be used to illustrate the ingredients of religious and political conversion.

Many of those ingredients have been highlighted by various authors. Zimbardo, in *Influencing Attitudes and Changing Behaviour*, establishes four influencing events to pay attention to in the context of sudden religious conversions: first, a close personal relationship needs to be developed with the people one wishes to convert to one's own position. It is human to respond to the offer of caring from another individual, to respond, especially if affection-starved and disoriented, to the tempting welcome into the bosom of a strong and loving family; second, the arousal of emotion by the leader, whether by emotional speeches, rhythmic music or dancing, serves to stir up troubling deep guilt and fear feelings in the audience which can be relieved quickly by submission to the cause; third, by responding to the appeal to come forward, to make promises or to speak out and be counted, people can be coaxed to commit themselves by actions which may then, as has been shown, colour their consequent attitudes; last, says Zimbardo, comes the powerful influence of prayer. The act of prayer may serve many purposes, in this context. It binds the group, acts as a reminder of the initial emotions experienced during the conversion itself, reinforces belief and, by focusing on the power of a supernatural force to bring good or evil, serves to place an individual's total responsibility for his actions outside himself. Prayer can bring peace, just as confession for Dr Vincent brought relief from all the aroused guilt, uncertainty and identity confusion he experienced in his Chinese prison. Whatever else may exist in the essence of prayer, prayer as a form is an effective instrument for manipulation.

Sargant has seen Evangelical-type conversion as a prime example of what can happen when the brain reaches overload and succumbs to a surfeit of stress. At the sermons of Wesley, for instance, it was a regular occurrence for people to collapse as the mass hysteria mounted, and to rise saved. Wesley's hell-fire speeches aroused the whole gamut of emotions in his audience, from guilt and fear to anger and indignation. It was irrelevant which. The result was physical collapse and an ensuing state of suggestibility which led to instant conversion. Sargant has a logical starting point for his discussions:

'Methods of religious conversion have hitherto been considered more from psychological and metaphysical angles than from physiological and physical ones; but techniques employed often approximate so closely to modern political techniques of brainwashing and thought control that each throws light on the mechanics of the other . . . Almost identical physiological and psychological phenomena may result from religious healing methods and conversion techniques, equally in the most primitive and the more highly civilised cultures. They may be adduced as convincing proofs of the truth of whatever religious or philosophic beliefs are invoked. But since those beliefs are often logically irreconcilable with each other and since the similarity of the physiological and psychological phenomena produced by their invocation are all that they may have in common – we find ourselves confronted with a mechanistic principle deserving the most careful examination.' (*Battle for the Mind.*)

Sargant may be alone in stressing the physiological side of conversion but many authors support the importance of psychological factors in the conversion syndrome.

Eric Hoffer, in *The True Believer*, makes the case that frustration is the key to understanding the sudden embrace of rigid religious belief:

'Starting out from the fact that the frustrated predominate among the early adherents of all mass movements and that they usually join of their own accord, it is assumed . . . that an effective technique of conversion consists basically in the inculcation and fixation of proclivities and responses indigenous to the frustrated mind.

'. . . Those who would transform a nation or the world cannot do so by breeding and captaining discontent . . . or by coercing people into a new way of life. They must know how to kindle and fan an extravagant hope.'

He explains why, in his view, faith offers so much to the frustrated:

'Faith in a holy cause is to a considerable extent a substitute for lost faith in ourselves. . . . The less justified a man is in claiming excellence for his own self, the more ready is he to claim all excellence for his nation, his religion, his race or his holy cause.'

Hoffer has mentioned, as quoted above, that the successful manipulator for a mass movement must play on those elements that are indigenous to the frustrated mind. He pursues that theme:

ıe frustrated more easily indoctrinated than the
ıstrated? . . . There is apparently some connec-
tween dissatisfaction with oneself and a proneness to credulity. The urge to escape our real self is also
an urge to escape the rational and the obvious. The
refusal to see ourselves as we are develops a distaste for
facts and cold logic. There is no hope for the frustrated
in the actual and possible. Salvation can come to them
only from the miraculous. . . . They ask to be deceived.'

Effective propaganda, then, cannot be forced on closed
minds. It can only work on what is already within. Rather
than impose new opinions, propaganda works if it articu-
lates forcefully and graphically nebulous passions and fears
and resentments that are constantly simmering below consciousness. Whereas Sargant's version of events, with the
accent on the physiological, allows the implantation of any
ideas, however alien, Hoffer believes the seeds for fervent
belief must have been already long sowed.

He names the family as the major threat to the success
of all mass movements. It is impossible to love one's
family above all and also to love one's movement above all.
Even for Christianity, Hoffer says, the family is a threat
because strong family ties are inconsistent with the concept of brotherly love for one and all. Therefore all mass
movements, including Christianity, have to aim to disrupt
family ties. In the Western world, where family links are
already weakened by economic factors, including economic
independence which allows women to contemplate divorce, children to go far from home, etc., the result has
indeed been the growth of a collective rather than family
spirit, says Hoffer.

If the family has become a less potent force in Western
industrial society, it has experienced an emotional renaissance recently, much nursed by the media, with the
advent of new religious cults imputed with the sinister
intent of 'breaking up the family'. It is because of these

same cults that the word 'brainwashing' has experienced a similar renaissance, possibly because the cults are new and therefore facilitate a focusing of attention which is more difficult to sustain in the case of long-established institutions which may, in fact, operate by similar means. It is worth, therefore, looking closely at the operative elements of modern-day religious cults.

Edward Schils, in an article called 'Authoritarianism: "Right" and "Left"', has analysed the features that were common to the Nazi and Russian systems. As it has already been suggested that all mass movements are interchangeable, it is to be seen whether these also apply to the religious cult. They are:

1. In-group exclusiveness and hostility to all outside it.
2. Demand for total submissiveness to the in-group which alone can bring about good.
3. The categorisation of people according to selected characteristics and making overall judgements on the basis of these (e.g. 'red scum', 'imperialist bastard').
4. Promotion of the idea that the world is a scene of unceasing conflict, e.g. as a result of 'class war'.
5. The view that any tenderness for family bonds or toleration of enemies serves only to weaken the in-group in its struggle and dilute commitment.
6. Belief in hostile conspiratorial forces whose aim is to destroy the in-group. Survival may therefore require violence.
7. Belief in a wholly harmonious society which can only be created by the in-group.

Cults

In March 1981, an English High Court jury decided that the Moonie cult does brainwash people, after hearing an action brought by the cult against the *Daily Mail* for making 'untrue' accusations about it. The jury heard much evidence about the nature of the cult, much of which is known to apply to others of similar ilk. The Moonie cult may therefore serve as an initial illustration of cult consciousness.

According to Reverend Sun Myung Moon, the leader of the Unification Church whose followers are colloquially known as the Moonies, God's intent was that Adam and Eve should marry and have perfect children. But Satan ruined things, Jesus failed to redeem things and it was now Moon's mission, as a prophet, to bring to the world the message of truth. The Moonies' role is to bring the world to Reverend Moon.

Moonie converts entrusted with the task take to the streets to give out leaflets or sell wares and encourage likely looking recruits to come to a week-end retreat to learn about what Moon has to offer. Sometimes it is not even made clear that the retreat is a Moonie venture, just a social gathering where the unsuspecting 'victim' can meet like-minded people. There are many accounts of what goes on at the introductory week-ends. Margaret Hyde described the process in *Brainwashing and Other Forms of Mind Control*.

Friday night, when the workshop/retreat started, there would be a simple dinner, followed by the singing of hymns, the playing of games and praying. Next day everyone had to get up early because every minute of the day was already programmed. The singing of hymns, chanting of prayers and the performing of exercises were all packed in before breakfast. Then came more hymns and a lecture, another hymn and another lecture on the sins of the world and how the Moon family had rejected Satan. More hymns, praying, lectures, simple games and, throughout, a great emphasis on the family's affection for all members and the strong group spirit. Those who were already Moonies, the 'brothers' and 'sisters', would demonstrate utter devotion to the group and strong will to conform to all required of them. One recruit is quoted as saying, 'You find yourself enjoying the feeling that you are accepted by the family, even wanted desperately by them. The prayers to save you are fervent.'

Recruits were free to leave at the end but by then they were likely to be in a state of confusion as a result of all the programmed action, the lack of sleep, the simple bland food and the cajolery from Moonie members to encourage them to stay. Leaving was not so simple a matter – yet, if they stayed, it would appear to them that they had made the *choice* to do so.

As part of an academic assignment, a student of Zimbardo's experienced such a Moonie week-end. From his own account in *Influencing Attitudes and Changing Behaviour*:

> 'After about six hours sleep I was awakened by a guitar, violin and two brothers filling the Chicken Palace with "The red red robin came bop-bop-bopping along . . ." Everyone rocketed out of their sleeping bags and into their clothes, shaking hands and asking, "How are you, brother?" "Great! Just Great!" was everyone's response. It was great to see everybody so happy. We all went out to the field and began singing: hand in hand or with arms around each other we formed a great circle. "Is everybody happy?" cried David, one of the leaders. "Yesss!!" screamed the crowd wildly. I believed it and let it flow into me. . . .
>
> 'After the exercises, discussion groups of thirteen were formed . . . Kristina (the discussion leader) then asked us, one by one, to discuss our life's goals and direction. All the family members talked about how they hadn't known what they wanted, how to change the world or how to be happy until they joined the family. . . .'

Dr Margaret Singer, a professor in the Department of Psychiatry of the University of California at Berkeley and a professor in the Department of Psychology at the University of San Francisco, gave evidence about the conversion techniques used by Moonies, at the London trial. Dr Singer worked as a research psychologist for the US army at the Walter Reed Army Institute of Research in Washington DC from 1952 to 1958. She worked with Edgar Schein at Walter Reed and herself conducted a five-year follow-up of 3,000 returned POWs from Korea. She told the court that she had personally interviewed more than 500 ex-cultists in America, about half of whom had been Moonies, and gave her opinion that the word 'brainwashing' was as good a word as any to describe the mind control techniques which, in her judgement, were practised by the Moonies and other cults down the ages. All had a basic pattern; refinements were made by individual cults to suit their particular needs.

She said in court: 'There is no doubt in my mind that of the many cults practising forms of brainwashing, the Moonies to a probably greater degree than any other cult rely upon all the essential features found in the indoctrination techniques that constitute brainwashing.'

The three basic techniques were the stripping process, the identification process and the final stage of rebirth. The cult, she said, used the stripping process to assault the identity of the new recruit, establish an atmosphere of outward peace and quiet, encourage the process of self-betrayal and lead to the breaking point where the recruit would renounce all his old life, including his family and personal goals, and embrace the cult and its teachings. By means of the identification process, the cult suppressed and punished past identities and rewarded and controlled the new emerging identity. The final stage was the death of the old self and rebirth as a Moonie.

She could see, at work in the Moonie process, she said, the three major elements of brainwashing that Lifton cited – the powerful togetherness of group identification, the closing in of the milieu with all the emotional conflict that ensues, and the culmination in total submission and rebirth. Also, however, her own work had led her to isolate five constant elements used in indoctrination by the Moonies. These she termed the five Ds.

Dependency   The recruit is suddenly cut off from family, friends and all that is familiar when he moves into the Moonie environment. Alienated from all that was his life, he comes to feel that he cannot survive away from the cult and therefore is drawn to commit himself to permanent involvement.

Dread   Coupled with the fear of failing to survive, unless he stays with the group, is the fear of losing group approval, love and affection, should he do anything wrong. Total alienation would then ensue.

Debilitation Members are kept so busy that they have no time to think about what they are doing and what they are being told. Weakness is caused by the long hours of work or lectures, little sleep and poor diet.

Deception Recruits are given a false picture of the cult when they are solicited on the streets. The cult may be described simply as a communal, loving group. Singer says she was told by some former cult leaders that they were instructed by senior Moonies to say whatever they thought would appeal to the new recruit most. So, if the recruit was carrying a guitar, it might be presumed he was interested in music and might be attracted by the idea of going along to a group of friendly people who all played and enjoyed music too. Fund raising was also achieved on the basis of deception.

De-sensitisation Moonies become programmed to feel nothing of the horror they might normally feel for acts they are required to do. Singer gives the example of their obtaining money by deception from people with little means and the grief inflicted on families by a child's involvement with the cult.

Singer isolated certain practices of the Moonies which served to achieve their ends. Recruits, for instance, were encouraged to think of the Moonies as their new family and to reject their old one, because the old family was a tool of Satan. Moonies had all aspects of their sexuality controlled so that they would not develop a loyalty to a particular boy or girl which might adversely affect loyalty to Moon.

Extremely strong emphasis was placed on 'sharing' – long sessions during which people were encouraged to talk about past hang-ups, while in the supportive environment of their group, and to exaggerate the significance of such feelings and the behaviour they prompted. Soul-baring brought approval, refusal to participate brought disapproval from the group.

Moonies were cut off from all 'outside' information, as put across in newspapers and on the radio and TV. They developed an in-language of their own and were implanted with trigger thoughts or phrases, such as, when fund raising, 'Bring in the money, bring in the people'. They were also implanted with the idea that anything negative they experienced was because of the evil still in them. Thus no blame could ever be attached to the Moonie cult itself. Even when the poor diet induced gastro-intestinal upsets about which members complained, they were told that the illness was a manifestation of the evil within them coming out.

New members were encouraged to spy on one another and report any backsliding or doubts to the older members. This led to distrust among new members and encouraged them to rely more heavily on the hardened converts. Confessions which had been extracted from members during 'sharing' sessions, often very intimate in detail, were often 'recalled' by senior Moonies if someone threatened to leave the group.

Trancelike states, leaving people extremely receptive to ideas and trigger words, were regular occurrences for people forced to sit for long hours on hard chairs listening to repetitive lectures. Running through all the teaching was the implicit promise that, by right behaviour, all members could be part of an élite that would eventually take over the world.

Most vulnerable to the Moonie approach, said Singer, were depressed and lonely people, or people who had just broken off from a relationship and were feeling rejected and insecure. Recruiters were often told specifically to go and look for lonely people and taught how to establish close eye contact with them while doing the sell.

Those cult members who did manage to escape or whose parents retrieved them tended to suffer long-term effects as a result of their indoctrination, Singer said. She mentioned trouble in concentrating, alienation, guilt about sex or guilt about deceptions they had practised as Moonies and anger about having been duped.

From this picture provided in court by Singer, it is easy to see the kinds of influence techniques, already described in this book, being applied wholesale by the Moonies.

In *Snapping*, an analysis of cults and conversion by Flo

Conway and Jim Siegelman, many quotations from cult
members themselves show those influences at work. For
instance, the power of repetitive activity and boredom to
induce a trancelike suggestible state is revealed in the words
of Cathy, a young Moonie who spent three hours in continual
prayer for the sake of new members: 'When I stood up, I felt
like thin air. I had to brace myself. I felt this energy, it was a
kind of ecstasy. It just flowed through me like a sensation of
tingling. It sent shocks through me. I equated it with divine
love.'

Lifton has spoken of thought-terminating clichés, Sargant
of the Chinese tactic of preventing questioning of Communism among the Chinese by fostering the idea that evil
thought is as bad as an evil deed. Cults have their own
methods to achieve not-thinking among cult members.

Again from *Snapping*, a Divine Light Mission member
says: 'The meditation Maharaj Ji was teaching involved
intensity, not depth. The intensity was the concentration
with which you focused on, say, the sound of your own
breathing. . . . It gave me a certain absence of feeling. It
eventually reached a point where, when I had doubts, guilt
or other uncomfortable emotions, I would immediately react
by meditating. After a while, any significant thought I might
have was immediately obliterated by meditating.'

Other cult members said that, in the same circumstances,
they might chant. One est graduate (est is the 'technique for
living' developed by Werner Erhard) told the authors of
Snapping that, in est, thinking is the enemy because it is the
barrier to experience. Thinking, he said, was just old tape
recordings going round and round, clogging the essence of
pure experience.

Jim Jones, leader of the People's Temple, who committed
suicide with his members in Guyana (at his own command)
was reputed to tell his followers that they must never ask *why*
he said something, just do it. Criticising or questioning him
weakened the power of the group.

Being 'forewarned' helped two Moonie members withstand pressure on their beliefs (see section on commitment in

Chapter 6): 'We had been told a lot of times people will get sucked back into the real world and Satan through their families and you had to cut that emotional tie and look at your parents objectively. Lawrence's mother got frantic when she realised we were going back; she ran out to the car crying, but we remained very cool and untouched by her. As we drove away, I said, "It must be very hard for you to see your mother like that." And Lawrence said, "That's not my mother, that woman who is crying and carrying on is not my real mother." And I was proud of him then, for seeing things the way they were.' (*Snapping*.)

Margaret Hyde in *Brainwashing* quotes an ex-member of the cult Children of God to demonstrate the cult's dependence on fostering the idea of all blame being internal:

> 'If one can be convinced that his/her own mind cannot be trusted and if one can be told often enough that any doubts and longings are the work of the devil, complete alienation from former supportive individuals may be accomplished. Along with the constant propounding of the cult's beliefs, an element of fear is reportedly introduced so that even though the converts are told they are free to leave, few do so.'

Californian Ted Patrick, who nearly lost his son to the Children of God, is now famous as a deprogrammer, someone who uses intensive tactics to break the hold of a cult on a recruit. He says that the main thrust of deprogramming is forcing people to *think*, to challenge them to answer questions for which they have not been programmed with an answer. The more frustrated they become, because they have been taught there is an answer to all attacks, the more they are forced to open their minds. The point suddenly comes when they can see what has happened to them and their minds start to function for themselves again. Patrick admits to using shock tactics sometimes, such as cutting off a Hare Krishna member's sacred pony tail, but says that most stories of his practices are exaggerated out of all proportion – and that helps. People who are 'kidnapped' from their cult and brought to him are terrified before he even starts on them. Fear of succumbing facilitates succumbing.

An ex-Evangelical preacher called Marjoe Gortner told a salutary tale to the authors of *Snapping* which goes far to confirm Zimbardo's statement that an illusion of invulnerability serves only to increase the ease with which one can be controlled.

Gortner saw his role as preacher as similar to that of a rock star. He would make a strong entrance, go through the old standard numbers and build up to his 'hit song' at the end, by which time the audience is in ecstasy. 'The people who are out there don't see it as entertainment although that is in fact the way it is.'

Now that he is no longer a preacher, Gortner spends much time trying to convey to the public the kinds of rhetorical techniques that are so commonly used to manipulate their thoughts and emotions. From *Snapping*:

'I lecture in about twenty colleges a year and I do a faith-healing demonstration – but I always make them ask for it. I tell them that I don't believe in it, that I use a lot of tricks; and the title of the lecture is "Rhetoric and Charisma", so I've already given them the whole rap explaining how it's done but they still want to see it. So I throw it all right back at them. I say, "No, you don't really want to see it." And they say, "Oh yes. We do, we do!" And I say, "But you don't believe in it anyway, so I can't do it." And they say, "We believe, we believe!" So after about twenty minutes of this I ask for a volunteer and I have a girl come up and I say, "So you want to feel better?" And I say, "You're lying to me! You're just up here for a good time and you want to impress all these people and you want to make an ass out of me and an ass out of this whole thing, so why don't you go back and sit down?" I really get hard on her and she says, "No, no. I believe!" And I keep going back and forth until she's almost in tears. And then, even though this is in a college crowd and I'm only doing it as a joke, I just say my same old line, "In the name of Jesus" and touch them on the head and, wham, they fall down flat every time!'

As Hoffer said, people so often ask to be deceived.

Schil's analysis of the features common to Russian and Nazi régimes seems very largely to apply also to religious cults. Even grandiose ideas about power and belief in hostile conspiratorial forces are all there. The Maharishi sent Transcendental Meditation teams out to countries undergoing strife in order to create a calming influence on the atmosphere. est established a Hunger Project to end world starvation. At the other end of the spectrum, the Hare Krishna group has collected together an arsenal for self defence, part of Moon's operation is the manufacture of rifles and ammunition and Synanon, the cult which started as a social programme to aid drug addicts, owns different types of guns and a vast amount of ammunition. But cults don't have to be vast and internationally based to get drunk on power, as the story of a very different cult, the Family, shows.

The Manson Family

In August 1969 seven people died a gruesome death at the hands of members of Charles Manson's Family. On Manson's instructions, Susan Atkins (Sadie), Patricia Krenwinkel (Katie) and Charles Tex Watson carried out the murder of Roman Polanski's wife, Sharon Tate, and three friends in her Los Angeles home, while a fourth Family member, Linda Kasabian, stood guard outside. The victims suffered between them 102 stab wounds and PIG was written on the door in Sharon Tate's blood. A visitor to the Polanski's caretaker, who got in the way, was shot four times and knifed. The next night Rosemary and Leno LaBianca were the victims, stabbed to death and attacked with a carving fork after death. The word WAR was scratched on to Leno's cheek and the words 'Death to Pigs' 'Healter Skelter' [*sic*] and 'Rise' were scrawled on the walls in Leno's blood. The killers that time were Charles Tex Watson, Leslie Van Houten and Katie.

When Manson and his followers were finally brought to trial, the Manson women who had not been involved kept vigil outside the courthouse. When Manson carved an X on his forehead, all his women followed suit. If he yelled out in court, the three women defendants got up and did likewise. It became clear that Manson had immense power over the women associated with him.

Vincent Bugliosi, the prosecutor, who later wrote the book of the case, *Helter Skelter* with Curt Gentry, commented on the Manson women: '. . . There was a little girl quality to them, as if they hadn't aged but had been retarded at a certain stage in their childhood. . . . Each was in her own way a pretty girl. But there was a sameness about them that was much stronger than their individuality, same expressions, same patterned responses, same tone of voice, same lack of distinct personality. The realisation came with a shock – they reminded me less of human beings than of Barbie Dolls.'

The issue became, had these girls been brainwashed? If so, they couldn't be held responsible for their conduct. Bugliosi wanted convictions, therefore it was up to him to show that the girls *were* responsible for their actions, however puppet-like they might have appeared. But the evidence that came out at the trial showed that Manson used power techniques with his Family members which by now should be all too familiar as effective coercive methods. The word 'brainwashing' left aside, it is worth reviewing Manson's tactics.

Charles Manson had a loveless youth and spent most of his life in institutions, including prison, until he was thirty-two. He had by this time developed an interest in hypnosis, Scientology, the occult and kindred subjects, about which he read extensively. He went to San Francisco at the height of flower-power and received love and lots of it for the first time in his life. But Manson couldn't just accept the love, he had to manipulate it. Very shortly he learned that women were mesmerised by him and he set about creating a Family over which he had total control. He convinced the Family that there would be a world war between blacks and whites and they had to take cover so that, when it was over, Manson could emerge as leader of the world. The war was known as 'Helter Skelter' and the brutal murders were an attempt to speed things up – they were supposed to be blamed on the Black Panthers.

The girls who were drawn in to the Manson fantasy had all had an insecure background. Either they had not got on with their parents or they had rejected parental values and were drifting alone, directionless, in the world.

Scheflin and Opton describe the 'initiation process' into the Family in *The Mind Manipulators*. Each woman had a very long initial sexual encounter with Manson:

> 'But it was not really the sex that was important – most of these women were hardened sexual veterans. It was the words before and during sex that mattered. With Susan Atkins, Manson had her pretend he was her father. If a woman was plain, he might tell her she was beautiful. If she were looking for a Godlike figure, he might imply that he was Jesus Christ. The crucial thing was that the woman had to make a quick and clean break with her past and this could most easily be done by focusing in on the most severe problem associated with her past and seemingly eliminating it. But what Manson really did was to *enhance* the problem and to continually use it thereafter as a method of adhesion.'

In other words, he probed till he found the source of each girl's deepest fears and played on it.

Manson also encouraged the familiar 'no thought' policy. He made all the decisions, even as to when people would eat, have sex and sleep. What people did between times was also up to Manson to decide. He encouraged the use of drugs, saying, 'When you take LSD enough times, you reach a state of nothing. Of no thought.'

Manson had read much about hypnotism and many family members concluded that he hypnotised them. Certainly he would make the most of eye contact and the power of soft monotonous tones to soothe people into suggestible states.

Sheflin and Opton quote one male ex-member who said, 'He would talk to you in a soft, soothing voice, like someone lulling you to sleep and even though he'd later suggest things that would seem impossible, yet you could not stop yourself – even if you were in a straight world, from going out and doing it.'

Every day, at every meal, Manson would reiterate his philosophies of life, indoctrination by the time-tested means of repetition. He knew well that, as they lived in seclusion as a family, his followers would receive no counter-information of any kind to conflict with the content of his own. He said it himself: 'They may not believe it 100 per cent but they can still draw opinions from it, especially if they have no other information to draw their opinions from.' (*Helter Skelter*)

Just as in the American naval programme to desensitise men to violence (Chapter 4), Manson accustomed his members to brutality by making them participate in bloody rites and in showing films of the events. A couple of men testified that they had seen films of Family members wielding knives and pretending to attack each other or films of a dog being sacrificed and its blood drunk.

While stirring up buried fears, exacerbating them with drugs, driving his followers to experience their deepest despair and uncertainty, all in the name of building their identities anew, Manson remained the 'friend', the source of comfort they could turn to, the one who understood. He was the one fixed point in a shifting world.

But Manson wasn't always love, even to his women. He beat them, threatened them, kept them in a state of fear which itself had holding power. Believing as they did in Helter Skelter, there was nowhere else for them to go for safety. Fear for their own future was Manson's ultimate weapon.

It must be pointed out that the authors of *The Mind Manipulators* reject the idea that the Manson women were brainwashed – or that Moonie converts were either. They maintain that charisma was the power element involved and that charismatic cults act as substitute families:

'It is no coincidence that charismatic cults so often refer to themselves as families: that is one of their main attractions. Where else in our society can a reluctant adolescent or post-adolescent put aside the anxieties of adulthood, regress to the total security of pre-pubescent childhood and also be flattered that he is wise beyond his years?

'When one sees cult members accept stultifying group pressures and demeaning discipline, it is tempting to suppose that they must have been brainwashed. But children, even terribly abused children, usually cling to their families, come what may. We suggest that the same dynamics hold devotees to their religious masters.'

But here again we are perhaps arguing semantics. By their own description of events in the Manson case, Scheflin and Opton show that the Family girls were subjected to considerable pressure, tailor-made to hit target – their most vulnerable inner selves. Whether they were coerced into belief or willingly abdicated the responsibility for thinking, in outcome they became subservient to Manson's will. They were victims of their own human need for affection, warmth, security, their human failings of guilt and fear and yearning for certainty in an uncertain world.

Patty Hearst

Sudden political conversions can be achieved in much the same sorts of ways that work for religious conversions. Induced emotional fervour commands the same rallying power, regardless of the end in mind. T. H. Qualter, in *Propaganda and Psychological Warfare*, describes how Hitler did it:

'Uniforms, bands, flags, symbols were all part of the German propaganda machine, designed by Hitler and Goebbels to increase the impact of strong words by evidence of strong deeds. Meetings were not just occasions for people to make speeches, they were carefully planned theatrical productions in which settings, lighting, back-

ground music and timing of entrances and exits were
devised to maximise the emotional fervour of an audience
already brought to fever pitch by an hour or more given
over to singing and the shouting of slogans.'

The same psychological principles which serve to keep the
religious convert converted also work to maintain the
cohesion of political groups. The psychologist Andrew
Molnar, who made an extensive study of the nature of
insurgent groups, concluded that two principles were vital
for the establishment and maintenance of group bonds. The
first is that action shapes attitudes. Therefore initiates tend
to be required to carry out an act that proves allegiance to the
cause. The second is conformity, which is ensured by self-
criticism sessions, long wearying abstract discussions which
exhaust participants, indoctrination sessions and, perhaps
unexpectedly, an accent on democracy within the group.
Individuals are allowed to have their say and therefore
believe that they are participating in decision-making (although the decision is likely to be made by the leader
anyway). By giving 'power' to people on committees the
same effect is achieved. The power only goes so far but it is a
sop to any divisive ambitions that may develop within the
group.

The most recent celebrated and contested case of political
brainwashing was that of Patty Hearst. People usually
appear to choose to join revolutionary groups or they choose
to attend the rallies where their emotions are whipped into
fervour. But Patty Hearst did not choose to be exposed to the
philosophy of the revolutionary party that kidnapped her.
Did she ever have the chance to exercise choice in the events
that ensued and culminated in her participation in attempted
armed robbery for political ends?

Patty Hearst, the daughter of the American millionaire,
was kidnapped from her flat in Berkeley, which she shared
with her fiancé, in February 1974. Three members of the
Symbionese Liberation Army knocked at the door, forced
their way in with guns and then dragged Patty away to a flat

in Daly city, where she was left, gagged and blindfolded, in a closet. She said at her trial that initially she didn't even know she was in a closet; she thought it was a coffin and that the plan was to bury her alive. Several times that night one of the revolutionary group threatened her with death if she tried to get away.

The next day one of the group, Cinque, told Patty that her parents had committed crimes against the people and that she was going to be tried for them by the 'people's court'. He kept questioning her about her family's financial affairs in such a way, she said in court, that she felt he knew all the answers already. Throughout this and the next day, members of the group made a point of impressing on her that it made little difference to them whether she was killed or not.

Patty spent 57 days in one closet or another. Shortly after the kidnap, she was made to demand on tape that her father meet the SLA's ransom demands. But she was being fed with information from the SLA that it was unlikely that the Hearst Corporation would come up with the money because her parents didn't care about her. Her mother was wearing a black dress. 'Everyone was talking about me like I was dead,' Patty said.

Although Patty remained blindfolded in the closet, the group started to talk to her about their revolutionary plans. They also told her that the huge food share-out for the poor, which was part of the ransom demand, had been a failure because the Hearsts weren't trying, they just wanted to provoke the SLA into murdering Patty.

They started to train her to use guns, in case the FBI forced their way into the flat. Still while she was in the closet, Patty testified, two of the SLA made her have sex with them. She didn't offer resistance.

A month later the group moved to a new address in San Francisco (Patty was taken in a rubbish can) and locked Patty once again in a closet. On April 1, they let her out at last and told her they were going to let her go. Just before that time, Cinque had spoken to her in the closet and told her that she in fact had the choice, she could go or she could stay and join their movement.

William Harris, one of the SLA, put it this way:

'We had to help Tania [Patty was given a new name] understand what it meant to each of us to be a guerilla so that she could bring it to a personal level in her own head. On her part, she had to convince us that she was being honest, objective and realistic. . . . At the last second before Tania took off her blindfold, Cinque reminded her that she could walk freely out of the door and that we would help her return to her family and friends. We all wanted Tania to stay but we wanted to make sure that she saw all her options and was making a strong choice with no regrets or indecision.' (*Chicago Tribune*, February 6, 1976.)

Patty decided to stay. In a manuscript which she later prepared with the two surviving SLA members, William and Emily Harris, she said that she had gradually started to feel sympathy with the SLA cause. At meals, at first, she had sat silent in her blindfold but after a while she started to join in the discussions and began to see the evil of US imperialism. She said that she opened her eyes and realised it was time to get off her ass.

Her story in court was different. She claimed she never really believed that she could make the choice to leave. She thought she was being tested and that, if she opted for home, she would die.

After her release from the closet, she made another tape in which she stated that she was now a member of the SLA and was renouncing her old life. A bank robbery plan was started on almost immediately. Patty, now Tania, was photographed holding a gun and standing in front of the SLA symbol. She was trained for her part in the proposed robbery and Cinque told her that she was to make a speech in the bank. (He knew there was a camera there.)

Patty duly appeared on film and, on another tape, took responsibility for the crime. She didn't, however, make the speech in the bank. She was told, she said, that the FBI would now shoot her on sight.

The SLA then moved to Los Angeles where military training and classes, in readiness for the revolution, hotted up. In May, two members, William and Emily Harris, were caught in the act of shoplifting from a sports shop. Patty, waiting in a car outside, fired her gun at the building several times to cover their escape. Next day all of the SLA but those three were killed when, during a battle with the police, a building caught fire and burned all those inside.

Patty stayed with the Harrises, travelling with them to San Francisco, where she was arrested sixteen months later in a flat in which she was living, some few miles away from the Harrises.

The question in the public mind was, why did she stay with the two lone survivors of the SLA when she had her chance then to escape? Why, in fact, had she acted to save them at the sports shop?

Patty said, in court, that the latter had been an automatic action – she had been trained to respond that way if trouble arose. She also said that the Harrises had planned to keep the SLA alive and wanted her with them. They said they would find and kill her if she escaped.

Patty and the Harrises travelled to New York and then Pennsylvania, where they worked on a book about the SLA. Patty's contribution was an interview the Harrises held with her (in which they told her what to say, she claimed) and an autobiographical section which was also edited.

During the sixteen months when Patty was 'free', she travelled apart from the Harrises sometimes and actually lived apart from them at the end, although she said she did that because she was frightened of them. She still considered escape attempts hopeless because the Harrises would find her.

When Patty was captured, she defiantly gave the revolutionary salute. By the time she was brought to trial, her position had changed. She stressed her fear of the SLA, not her sympathy. She explained almost all actions as having been done because she knew she was supposed to do them. She even smiled, she said, because she was supposed to smile, so that she would look more like her media photographs and therefore be the more recognisable.

The defence called upon the 'brainwashing experts', psychiatrists who had studied the repatriated POWs, to back up their case that Patty wasn't responsible for her actions. Louis Jolyon West found similarities between the pressures put on Patty and those to which the POWs had been subjected, particularly disorientation, fear, dread, hopelessness. Just as the POWs were led to believe that no one at home cared or wrote, so Patty was imbued with the information that her parents considered her as good as dead and had no further interest in her.

Lifton gave the opinion that Patty's compliance was inevitable under the circumstances and that compliance can continue beyond the time of actual coercion. Lifton said that Patty had undergone all the emotional upheaval experienced by the POWs, induced in them by their captors: the helplessness, the identity assault, surfacing of buried guilt, humiliation, self-betrayal through confession, relief as a result of confession, gratitude for a show of leniency which then catapulted the prisoner into an eagerness to comply in a thirst for survival, to which, for the first time, he can see his way. Both West and Lifton found Patty to be suffering the same kinds of neurotic reactions after her arrest that the POWs experienced on repatriation.

Witnesses for the prosecution tried to show that Patty did act of her own free will when she participated in the bank robbery. Psychiatrist Dr Joel Fort, who had studied many kidnap victims, drew attention to the fact that Patty had not been a dutiful daughter. She had been independent, rebellious, rejected Roman Catholicism (her family's religion), took drugs and moved in with a man of whom her family was not too fond. He described her as an all-or-nothing sort of person, the very type whom Eric Hoffer has described in *The True Believer*. She was more similar to than different from the SLA, most of whom had come from standard middle class backgrounds and most of whom had come to feel dissatisfaction with their lives, just as Patty did. The SLA, to Patty, offered meaning in life, just as it had come to offer meaning to its members.

Patty did get convicted by that court although whether the jury understood, in the face of conflicting expert evidence, how to decide whether she was brainwashed or not, cannot be known. What is interesting to consider, however, is that the evidence from defence and prosecution hardly cancel each other out, they reinforce each other. Whatever the circumstances, Patty did not appear to make decisions that emanated wholly from within. Dissatisfaction and uncertainty about one's life would seem to be a strong disposing factor for leaving an individual in an all too ready state to embrace something new, something that can provide the answer and eliminate uncertainty once and for all. A decision made under such circumstances is no more informed than a decision overtly enforced. The question to ask is what constitutes a truly self-willed action? Toch has described (see Chapter 3) how the process of socialisation, where values inculcated from childhood are reinforced by the type of people one meets as a result of holding those values, prevents one from learning to cope with the ambiguities of life. In a world where everything is black *or* white, where 'if you are not part of the solution, you are part of the problem', sudden conversion of any kind should be known as a norm not an oddity.

In a previous chapter it has been discussed how elements such as the need to resolve cognitive dissonance or actions being sufficient to affect attitudes can influence behaviour. Patty 'acted' in the bank robbery. She had to square that with her conscience. She was made to speak on tape and write things down, thus participating in her conversion. She apparently made a 'choice' to stay with the SLA, therefore she would have had to resolve the conflict involved (if there were indeed conflict) by coming to believe in the rightness of that choice. She was a non-conformist type, it was agreed, before her capture. Therefore, having conformed to her captor's view of life, it was perhaps to be expected that she would need to embrace it the more fully (to resolve cognitive dissonance).

It might therefore be said that everything in Patty's life, from her upbringing and unresolved emotions to the actual events of her kidnap experience, pointed her in the direction that she took.

In *The Mind Manipulators* Scheflin and Opton reject the brainwashing explanation whenever it is applied:

> '. . . Brainwashing is more than a scareword. It is also a strangely *attractive* idea. . . . We do not want to confront Pogo's famous insight, "We have met the enemy and he is us". How much more comforting to think, "We have met the enemy and he is Satan" or "she is a witch" or "his mind is possessed by demonic spirits" or "he has been brainwashed by the Communists" or "by the Moonies" or "by the Symbionese Liberation Army". Thus the idea of brainwashing paralyses thought because it places responsibility somewhere else.'

But it might equally well 'paralyse thought' to insist on attributing inexplicable action to consciously willed motives. To reject the idea of brainwashing means, in its widest sense, to reject the idea that we are ever out of control of our own actions. For to admit we can be swayed and manipulated is possibly more frightening than to admit that others can choose to perform socially or politically or morally unacceptable actions.

9 THE PROFESSIONAL AT WORK

In *Coercive Persuasion* Edgar Schein said: 'There is a world of difference in the content of what is transmitted in religious orders, prisons, educational institutions, mental hospitals and thought reform centers. But there are striking similarities in the manner in which influence occurs.' This chapter looks at some of those similarities.

The Police

One of the famous cases in English criminal annals is that of the Christie murders. By the time Christie was convicted of murdering several people, another man had already been hanged for allegedly killing two of them. Timothy Evans' 'confession' was completely fictitious although it was made in all sincerity at the time. Since Evans' posthumous pardon from the crimes, it has become familiar to see items in national newspapers concerning the eliciting of confessions by police by means of pressure. One more recent example was the Confait case, where three boys of subnormal intelligence confessed to the murder of homosexual Maxwell Confait, and were later found to be totally innocent.

How can anyone be pressured, without physical torture, into confessing to so serious a crime as murder (aside from those whose existential guilt or particular neuroses leads them to make unlikely confessions to any crime)? Though there are those who will claim that some policemen force confessions that they know are untrue, because they want their conviction, the Evans case, to be discussed shortly, showed that sometimes both parties can be equally deceived by events that overtake them.

Sargant believes that if the right kind of stress is induced in the interview room, breakdown of the suspect is inevitable and confession elicited, whether it is true or not:

'To elicit confessions, one must try to create feelings of anxiety and guilt and induce states of mental conflict if these are not already present. Even if the accused person is genuinely guilty, the normal functioning of his brain must be disturbed so that judgement becomes impaired. If possible he must be made to feel a preference for punishment – especially if combined with a hope of salvation when it is over – rather than a continuation of the mental tension already present or now being induced by the examiner. Whenever guilty persons make "voluntary" confessions to the police against their better interests, thus earning sentences of imprisonment or death, and the evidence suggests that physical violence has not been used, it is interesting to enquire whether one or more of the four physiological methods have been used which were also found by Pavlov to succeed in breaking down the resistance of animals.' (*Battle for the Mind*)

The questions that need to be asked, he says, are whether the police examiners deliberately provoked anxiety; whether they prolonged the stress to a point where the man or woman couldn't function normally any longer and became increasingly suggestible as a result; whether the suspect was so confused by changing attitudes, changing examiners, and question upon question that he lost his orientation and was led to incriminate himself; and whether any additional measures were used to weaken the suspect physically (perhaps long hours of questioning) so that his system eventually had to succumb to the combined pressures on him.

Ludovic Kennedy, a great believer in Timothy Evans' innocence, wrote *Ten Rillington Place*, published in 1961, in an effort to get his conviction investigated. He believes that Evans' treatment and experience in custody induced the emotions which Hinkle and Wolff found resulted from the treatment to which American POWs were subjected in Korea. The result in both cases was extreme suggestibility.

Kennedy retells the Evans story, accenting the points along the way which seemed to indicate a 'brainwashing' experience.

Evans and his wife Beryl had been living in a house where Christie and his wife were also tenants. Christie had impressed upon the pair that he had medical experience and when Beryl became pregnant again (she had one child) and wanted an abortion, he had offered to see to it for her. Evans was very against the idea of an abortion but eventually he had to acknowledge it was going to go ahead. He even told Christie as he left for work on the fateful day that Beryl was ready for him. When Evans returned home, he learned the news that Beryl was dead, because, as he believed, the operation had been a failure. (In fact Christie had strangled her and had sex with her after death, which had been his real intent.) He helped Christie store the body out of sight, not wishing to get Christie or himself into trouble over an illegal abortion. Evans was of subnormal intelligence. It made sense to him when Christie advised him to leave the house and let him, Christie, arrange with some people he knew to look after Geraldine, the other child. Christie told Evans he would dump the body down the drain. In fact he put it in the washhouse, together with the body of the child when he killed her too, expecting to bury both in the garden along with other corpses he had deposited there.

Evans went to stay with an aunt in Wales. But he was in a strange state, giving conflicting stories as to Beryl and the baby's whereabouts, and worrying himself about what had happened and how his child was and where. He dearly loved his daughter. Eventually, in desperation to find out about his child, he went to the police. He had decided to tell them that his wife had died of an abortion and that he himself had stuffed the body down the drain. He didn't think that this would be seen as a crime.

Kennedy points out that Evans was therefore already in a state of *anxiety* when he went to the police. In fact, it was to put an end to the intolerable anxiety that he went to them in the first place. Then came the intolerable *suspense*. Evans was kept in Merthyr Tydfil police station while London police went to investigate the specified drain. They found nothing, of course. But they did find two bodies in the washhouse Evans was therefore transferred to Notting Hill police station in London. This occurred 54 hours after he had first gone to the Welsh police. All of that time he had had no understanding of why he was being held. He had no idea that Beryl's body would not be found in the drain, and that she had met death through strangulation, not a botched abortion. Kennedy says that he did, however, suffer the equivalent of Hinkle and Wolff's *awareness that he was being avoided*. He was kept in solitary confinement in Wales and the journey under guard to London was made in virtual silence.

By this time he was certainly experiencing *feelings of unfocused guilt*. He knew that, if he had been firm, he could have stopped Beryl having her abortion and then she would have been alive. In a sense, he *had* therefore killed her, in his own mind. With time on his hands and only his anxieties about what had happened and what was happening now to occupy his mind, the formless guilt worked on him. He was full of guilt, but not guilty. Kennedy comments: 'It is a well known psychological fact that people suffering from an acute sense of guilt deliberately seek out punishment as a means of expunging it.'

Evans was also suffering the requisite amount of *fear and uncertainty*. He was terrified of Christie, terrified of what Christie would do if he thought his part in the death would come to light. Evans also expressed the fear later that the police might knock him about if he didn't make a statement that satisfied them.

The next step in Evans' downfall, as Kennedy enumerates them, was *bewilderment* of a very powerful kind. 'It is astonishing,' says Kennedy at this stage, 'how closely the events that accidentally happened to Evans follow the Communist pattern of interrogation.' The POWs reached a stage where they had to confess, if only for their own relief, but the Communists knew that the confession itself would not for long be convincing to the individual who made it. Therefore they would reject it. The POW who believed he had finally offered what was wanted of him was as a result completely bewildered and thrown into confusion anew. It would become all the more urgent for him to have his confession accepted, therefore he would invest more of himself in it, willing it unwittingly to be real. In Evans' case, he had made a confession. He had buried his wife in a drain. The police rejected it. He did not know they had reason to reject it, as he genuinely thought himself that his wife's body would be found in the drain. Only later was he hit with the accusation that, far from pushing his already dead wife down the drain, he had strangled both her and Geraldine and left both bodies in the washhouse. It was the first he knew of Geraldine's death. He had believed her alive in West London.

That he suffered *increasing depression, fatigue and despair* was self-evident. He also wanted to talk and therefore was dependent on his interrogators. The Communists deliberately altered their attitude from hostility one moment to friendliness the next in order to confuse the prisoner. For Evans such confusion also occurred because he had two police examiners, one whom he liked and the other who frightened him.

His increasing suggestibility and his need to confess, in order to achieve *relief*, led Evans to mistake the cause of the relief he felt after confession. He didn't realise that he had acted to dissipate his emotions, he presumed he had unburdened himself of his crime. He even said, 'It's a great relief to get it off my chest. I feel better already.'

That relief didn't last. In prison, the day after the hearing in the magistrate's court, he was able to tell his mother that he hadn't killed his wife and daughter. Christie had done it.

Also working against Evans in his interrogation was the genuine belief of the examining officers that Evans was indeed guilty.

'Indeed,' says Kennedy, 'it was the very intensity of their beliefs that blinded them to things they might otherwise have seen. Do not let us forget that on that very morning [of the investigation] Jennings [one of the officers] had seen with his own eyes the pathetic little bundle that was Geraldine lying behind the washhouse door.'

One of the things they might 'otherwise have seen' was the true nature of a piece of evidence which proved beyond doubt that Evans could not have put the bodies in the washhouse on the day he 'confessed' to putting them there.

Over the period of time in question, building work was being carried out at Ten Rillington Place. The evidence of the building works manager, the plasterer and the plasterer's mate, who had gone in and out of the washhouse, showed that no body could have been there on the date it was supposedly deposited (before Evans' departure to Wales). The wood that was found covering them had not even been given – to Christie – until a week later. The police officers were so convinced of Evans' guilt that at no point did their minds turn to wondering about Christie's role in all of this. Instead, they called in the builders and interrogated them all separately. The builders were obliged to wait for hours before they were seen and were then grilled for lengthy periods. The outcome was that the men eventually conceded that they must have been mistaken about the dates. (A time sheet that showed quite clearly the truth of the first statements and which had been given to the police was never seen again. It is the only time sheet missing from the firm's records over the relevant five-year period.)

In *Mental Seduction and Menticide*, Meerloo makes the point that 'those "charming" characters who are easily able to influence others are often extremely susceptible to suggestion themselves'. Sargant makes the same point for a different reason when he explains how confessions can come to be believed by both suspect and accuser:

'This is because the examiner first suggests to the prisoner that he is guilty of a crime and tries to convince him, if he is not already convinced, that this is so. Even if the prisoner is innocent, the long tension to which he has been subjected may well have already frightened him into suggestibility and if he is an unstable type he may then accept the examiner's view of his guilt. If the examination is pressed, he may even begin, as it were, to play back an old record – confessing to crimes suggested by the police in earlier cross-examinations. The police, forgetting that the incidents were originally their own guess-work, are deceived; the prisoner has now "spontaneously" confessed what they have been suspecting all along. It is not usually realised that fatigue and anxiety induce suggestibility in the examiner as well as the prisoner – the task of eliciting confessions is a very difficult and trying one – and that they can delude each other into a belief in the genuineness of the confessed crime.'

Meerloo explains such a phenomenon by the fact that the interrogation process induces a hypnotic state in the suspect. The suspect is able to produce bits and pieces of the confession wanted from him because 'the passive memory often remembers facts learned under hypnosis better than those learned in a state of alert consciousness'.

Kennedy says that, in such a way, Evans certainly succeeded in brainwashing *his* examiners: 'What Jennings and Black [the police officers] gave to him, he gave back to them and not only to them but to others in positions of even greater authority.'

Zimbardo points out that the American police have used psychology to refine their interrogation techniques not, of course, to elicit false confessions but in the belief that such tactics will uncover true ones from otherwise intransigent subjects. He lists the categories these tactics fall into: the environment is manipulated so that it denies the psychological support offered by any element of familiarity. Ideally there should be no ashtrays nor even a telephone; the suspect's perception of the crime is manipulated – he may be led to believe it isn't very serious; the relationship between interrogator and suspect is manipulated – the interrogator may stand over the suspect or demonstrate disquieting composure in the face of the suspect's unease. He may also play on the suspect's needs in order to establish a relationship, for example, by flattering an insecure person or playing up in himself characteristics which he believes the suspect admires; the interrogator also learns to manipulate words, charging them with the required emotion or using words like 'mother' which can elicit certain emotions. All weak points are carefully exploited.

Unfortunately, all such tactics, designed to enable an interrogator to get to the truth of a matter, can equally well operate to obscure it.

In England, it is now illegal for the police to interrogate a mentally handicapped person without an independent witness present. While that is an advance, a concession to the fact that a person of subnormal intelligence can be manipulated, even unintentionally, into confessing what is not the case, it almost, by very omission, implies that a person of normal intelligence could *not* be forced into a similar trap.

Psychotherapy

The tools of traditional psychiatry – drug régimes and physical treatments, such as electric shock therapy – are eschewed by very many modern practitioners of the art of emotional healing. Drugs, they say, are simply palliatives, not cures, for mental illnesses, designed to get people functioning again but not designed to elicit the emotional problems which caused the breakdown in the first place. Psychotherapy, on the other hand, works to free a patient to face and resolve his real, underlying problems, to experience a crisis and come through it instead of deadening the agony with drugs. Psychotherapy, then, is the treatment of choice for the liberal-minded doctor. In a free, uncritical environment, with his doctor's support, the patient can truly come to terms with himself.

Or can he? Many researchers have shown that psychotherapy is in fact a coercive process, the most 'acceptable' form of coercion perhaps but no less coercive for it.

In 1955 Rosenthal published a study called 'Changes in some moral values following psychotherapy' in a psychological journal. He was able to show that patients who were rated as having 'improved' by their therapists had, during therapy, changed their values in areas such as sex, aggression and authority in the direction of those held by their therapists on such matters.

Perry London comments on the occurrence in *Behaviour Control*:

'There is some evidence . . . . in research reports that patients tend to identify with their therapists, gradually developing similar personal values. It is no wonder that they should. For no matter how tentatively he approaches the patient, nor how pure his motives *not* to control or dominate, the insight therapist cannot help but address what he himself considers the most salient material presented to him. Eventually the patient's ideas of salience must largely correspond to his or the interaction cannot continue. What is more, the inherent balance in the relationship, where one person is always helping and the other receiving help, makes the patient look up to the therapist as a potential authority, model or inspiration, no matter how little he knows of the therapist's outside life. Almost inevitably he knows plenty about the therapist's attitudes towards the things that count most in his own life and it is those attitudes that he is most likely to absorb.'

One explanation for this effect has already been given in Chapter 4. The therapist unconsciously conditions the patient's response by nodding approval to certain things he says and ignoring or expressing mild disapproval of others. In this way, he guides the patient towards the areas he himself thinks valuable to talk about and to concentrate on words or ideas which have importance for *him*. It is an old joke (and a true one) that the patients of Jungian therapists dream Jungian dreams while the patients of Freudian therapists faithfully produce Freudian ones.

Sargant sees the anxiety which a patient brings with him to psychotherapy, and has exacerbated during therapy as part of the self-discovery process, as the vital element which, by building up to a level of intolerable stress, creates suggestibility in the patient.

As he describes psychoanalysis, a patient may have to lie on a couch perhaps daily for months, 'free associating' (saying whatever comes into his head). The therapist may then pick up on particular words and say, 'what does "ladder" mean to you? What significance does the word "nurse" have for you?' If the words are found to hold some sexual significance, the patient is then invited to go back over his sexual past and relive all and any incidents which aroused equivalent anxiety/anger/guilt/fear, etc. As some of the incidents may have happened in childhood and had been repressed till now, because they were so anxiety-inducing, the patient suffers ever-mounting stress and discomfort. The effort of reliving and re-experiencing is also exhausting. As the tension increases, so does the patient's dependence on his therapist and his initial resistance to the latter's interpretations of his actions is worn down. The patient comes to accept – and act upon – theories about his personal condition which may well be at variance with what he had always believed. He achieves 'insight'.

Stories about subtle shaping of behaviour during therapy abound. One woman was asked by her analyst whether she found herself looking between men's legs when she travelled on the London tube. The woman said no. On her way home, she found herself staring between the legs of men sitting opposite her on the train – and carried on doing so whenever she got on a train after. The therapist would probably have said that she had always wanted to sneak a peek and till now the desire had been repressed. Others might say he had suggested an idea which took hold and then became habit.

Frank says that the very nature of psychotherapy attracts people who will best respond to it, i.e. those who readily adapt their behaviour according to subtle direction. People who go to psychotherapy are those who have problems which result from their ability to respond to other people in an emotional way. They are touched by their relationships with partner, parents or colleagues to such an extent that they react emotionally to the interpersonal problems that arise, and in a way that induces sufficient stress to warrant 'treatment'. They are therefore highly susceptible to interpersonal influences – including those emanating from the analyst. There is evidence, says Frank, that suggestible people tend to stay in treatment longer than less suggestible people. Those who opt to enter therapy not because of any immediate distress which is affecting their lives but because of a calm wish to explore themselves more fully, do less well in therapy than those who readily experience anxiety on the couch.

Frank also suggests that therapists who go out of their way to make no responses that could influence the client's ability to express himself fully and freely may in actuality be exerting more influence than their less restrained colleagues:

'The therapist's steadfast refusal to assume active leadership tends to create an ambiguous situation for the patient, who has only a vague idea of what he is supposed to do, how long he is to keep it up and how he will know when he is finished. In response to the patient's attempts to gain clarification the therapist does nothing at all or may make non-committal encouraging sounds or ask non-committal questions. The resulting unclarity of the situation may enhance its influencing powers . . . . Everyone constantly tries to form stabilized and clear assumptions by which to guide his behaviour. Therefore a person in an ambiguous situation is impelled to try to clarify it, that is, to assume the initiative in trying to find out what is expected of him and then do it . . . .

'To the extent that a person cannot unaided construct a clear set of expectations in a situation, he tends to look to others for direction. This may explain the finding that confusion increases suggestibility. In evocative therapy, the patient's tendency to scrutinise the therapist for clues as to what is expected of him may be heightened by his belief that relief from his suffering depends on his doing or saying the right thing.'

Therefore the patient, in his desperate search for clues, is acutely aware of every movement the therapist makes. He unconsciously uses the therapist's own body language to help him construct a picture of how he should be performing.

Other social forces are also playing their part in the therapist/patient relationship. The patient has chosen to come to the therapist, therefore he has imbued the therapist with a certain degree of power – he believes the therapist can help him and has the knowledge and experience to do so. The therapist is an 'expert'. The patient's ingrained duty to obey and respect people in authority makes him unwilling to cross the therapist or to forfeit his approval.

In one sense, psychotherapists have a power akin to that of cult leaders. Because they are not concerned with the realm of the rational and the provable, their statements cannot be disproved and therefore comfortably rejected. A therapist can say, 'Your unconscious is making you do such and such' or 'In your unconscious mind you feel such and such' and the patient's conscious mind cannot plausibly show that to be untrue. A cult leader can say, 'You will only come to understand if you believe such and such' and the confused follower will never be sure whether he would have reached enlightenment if he had followed the route prescribed. Both patient and follower have to make judgements about whether they go along with such interpretations which pertain to the irrational but they only have their rational minds with which to make their judgement. Their only option, therefore, is to believe or not to believe.

The patient in psychotherapy is provided with a safe environment in which to 'confess' the secrets of his guilty past. But even more powerful is the confession made in group therapy where, as his reward, the patient experiences the admiration, approval and warmth of the other members of his group.

In an encounter group, for instance, each member may have his or her turn to work through some emotional block. One man may have felt hostility towards his mother for years and he can't understand it, because she has always been supportive and warm, with his best interests at heart. Persuaded at last to pretend that his mother is the pillow which he is handed and to thump that pillow and let his real feelings out, he discovers that he hates her because she never let him learn his own way and make mistakes for himself, she was always there protecting him. When his outburst is over, he feels freed from a huge burden. Bright-eyed, the rest of the group congratulate him on becoming himself at last. They feel proud that with their support he has let himself go and show him much affection and physical warmth to reaffirm how much more of a worthy person he seems to them now. Not only does the man experience the relief of expressing his tensions but he earns the social approval of his peers. He feels bound to them because they shared with him his deepest feelings, he feels gratitude and love. He may never have met them before. And, were he to be in a relationship with one of them, he might well be experiencing and repressing the very kinds of negative emotions – hostility, envy, insecurity – that he has expressed in front of them and been rewarded for. Yet the emotional atmosphere and the safe, sheltered environment leaves him feeling only love and trust.

A more intense experience of the same ilk occurs on est weekends. est (always spelt in lower case because supposedly that, like est itself, is not pretentious) is a technique designed to change the quality of life. Developed by ex-salesman Werner Erhard, it is not a therapy nor a religion. In groups of 250, over a long week-end spent sitting, for much of the time, on hard seats and with the minimum of breaks to go to the bathroom or eat, the participants are worked on by the trainers to realise that they are wasting their lives trying to live up to expectations of what they should be instead of accepting that they are what they are, that what is happening now is of their own making and that there is nothing to try to 'be' anyway. Individuals are invited to 'share' experiences and griefs which the trainer will then knock down and ridicule in an effort to make the person see what a mess he is making of his life. Attacks can be aggressive enough to make people vomit (vomit bags are provided), and get headaches and backaches. The participants carry out special exercises designed to make them see – and like – themselves for what they are. Most eventually 'get' it, the est word for insight. At the end of the week-end, after sharing all the public humiliation and personal anxiety and stress, participants commonly feel a tremendous warmth towards and bond with each other. Many people feel they have a radical new perspective on their lives, one that is shared by the 'in-group' (the est graduates) and not by the 'out-group' (everyone outside).

Elements of est are obviously very similar to the Chinese mode of thought reform, particularly in the revolutionary colleges where students were obliged to confess their sins and experience public humiliation. They interpreted their relief after confession as proof of the rightness of the new way.

Such group methods seem to generate not independence from a certain debilitating emotional block but dependence on the environment where the block was unblocked. Very many people become group habitués, seeking the warmth that comes from soul-baring. est graduates can attend more and more courses, although it might be wondered that if they had 'got' it the first time, why do they have to come back and 'get' it again? Or, more pertinently, what is it that they are really 'getting' in the first place?

The therapeutic environment, traditional or modern, would seem not to be influence-free. The *modus operandi* can generate specific emotions or encourage specific reactions. Behaviourist B. F. Skinner goes even further and maintains that, even if therapy could be influence-free, it would merely foster the illusion that a client was 'self-directing'. In a dialogue with Carl Rogers, he responds to Rogers' claim that client-centred therapy (where the client expresses exactly what he likes and the therapist simply listens) is the answer to therapeutic control:

> 'What evidence is there that a client ever becomes truly *self*-directing? What evidence is there that he ever makes a truly *inner* choice of ideal or goal? Even though the therapist does not do the choosing, even though he encourages "self actualisation" he is not out of control as long as he holds himself ready to step in when occasion demands –when, for example, the client chooses the goal of becoming a more accomplished liar or murdering his boss. But supposing the therapist does withdraw completely or is no longer necessary – what about all the other forces acting upon the client? Is the self-chosen goal independent of his early ethical and religious training? Of the folk wisdom of his group? Of the opinions and attitudes of others who are important to him? Surely not. The therapeutic situation is only a small part of the world of the client. From the therapist's point of view it may appear to be possible to relinquish control. But the control passes not to a "self" but to forces in other parts of the client's world. The solution of the therapist's problem of power cannot be *our* solution, for we must consider *all* the forces acting upon the individual.'

The Hard Sell

Advertising, by its nature, is designed to influence. While that is no surprise, the industry has taken itself increasingly seriously over the last decade, trying to find new, more effective and more subtle ways to sell the products it is paid to sell. Some of the appeals that are made through advertising aim for the same emotional weak spots that have been seen to make people vulnerable to influence in other, unrelated spheres.

There is, for instance, the familiar appeal of authority figures. Men in white coats eulogise the virtues of a particular denture cleaner or cough medicine because they summon up associations with doctors and scientists, professional men who know what they are talking about.

If many people who watch advertisements believe they are immune to such rather transparent sales tactics, are they as immune to the same 'sell' when it is used by newspapers? If a journalist is writing an article about gossip or the sex appeal of hair preparations, he is quite likely to ring (or to be told by his editor to ring) a psychologist or psychiatrist for an 'informed opinion' on why gossiping can be a useful thing to do or why certain smells on the hair can be sexually arousing. The psychologist or psychiatrist who finds himself on the end of the telephone talking to the journalist may well have no particular expertise on the matter (as why should he?) but will probably be willing to offer some common-sense suggestion that an insurance salesman, an architect or the journalist himself could just as easily have supplied. However, because the words were said by a psychiatrist or psychologist, who is expert in knowing how people tick, the sentiments take on an acceptable ring of authority, acceptable to the journalist, editor and the people who read it.

Who is to say, therefore, whether the advertisement viewer unconsciously endows the white-coated promoter of cough mixture with expertise worthy of respect. The housewife who promotes cough mixture can only say her children like it and get well quicker, etc. we will not let *her* get away with saying, 'I know this works because I tested it in the laboratories'.

Superficially, adverts can be seen to appeal to the universal thirst for social approval, provided by having a car, house, freezer, stereo system or draught-proofing that is at least as good as but preferably better than one's neighbours'. But much more goes into the planning of advertisement strategies than capitalisation on people's acquisitive instincts. Advertising is almost a science. Vance Packard describes the growth in sophisticated advertising adjuncts in *The People Shapers*. First came demographics, whereby the population is segmented according to age, income, education, occupation, ethnic background, size of family, etc., in order to identify the best prospects for a product. But that was not refined enough, says Packard:

> 'Today many ambitious marketers consider demographics just the beginning. They call next for "psychographics". Enter the behavioural specialists.'

The behavioural specialists then build psychological profiles of each target group. This time people are grouped according to their interests, life-styles, status aspirations, self-image, attitudes and fears and prejudices.

Alan R. Nelson, one enthusiast of psychographics that Packard mentions, discovered that the best way to sell decorated toilet paper (hardly an essential in life) was to make the most of a finding that guests instinctively study bathrooms to pick up information about their hosts. The bathroom, therefore, takes on new import. It is almost the soul laid bare. Any minor weakness an individual may have will most likely be betrayed by its manifestation in the bathroom. Decorated toilet paper was concluded to be one good solution to this dilemma of modern life.

Not all examples of the advertising psychologist at work are so amusing, or perhaps harmless. One consultant told a toy manufacturers' convention that their advertising should be geared towards stirring up the guilt of working parents. If both parents were out at work all day, they were likely to feel nagging worries that perhaps they were neglecting their child and would need to find ways to help square their conscience. How better than to buy the child special treats? The consultant said that such guilt could be exploited all year round. It didn't have seasonal limitations, like Christmas.

Successful attitude-influencers, in whatever context they are working, need to discover what it is that motivates individuals most, either to take steps to achieve something or to avoid something. Just as the Chinese and police interrogators have to discover the basic personality traits and weaknesses of *individuals* and tailor their technique to home in on them, so advertising at its most sophisticated must analyse prospective markets into ever-refined categories for the same purpose. It is not enough to aim at girls over fourteen but under 21; better to focus on fourteen to 21-year-olds who come from strict homes, are bothered about their weight and feel guilty about self-indulgence, and pitch the sales-talk accordingly. Just as confession may bring relief from anxiety, so may buying a particular product.

While it might be comfortable to believe that advertisers are probably not half so successful in their sell as they like to think they are, it is worth remembering that an audience may well aid the advertisers by its will to be deceived. Although the message has been put across *ad nauseam* by doctors (in consultations and in magazine columns) that there is no way to lose weight except to diet, every new fad pill or slimming machine that purports to shift inches is gratefully seized on by the overweight, in their desperation to find a solution that removes responsibility from themselves. Much product appeal is based on the fact that *you* don't have to make the effort to achieve the required results.

Adverts do not have to be subtle in content in order to be subtle in effect. By pure repetition, an association may be conditioned between a brand name and a product, in some cases with such success that the brand name becomes interchangeable with the product. Thus we talk about hoovers, xerox machines and biros.

If advertisers can encourage belief in their brand, they are probably home and dry. Belief in the name may be enough to make it work. Doctors at Keele University tested the effect of branding on 835 women who frequently suffered from headaches. The women were given either a particular well-known analgesic or placebo. Some of the women received the analgesics in a packet with the brand name on it, others received them in packets without a name. The placebos were also distributed in brand-name or no-name packets.

The doctors found that the greatest headache relief was provided by the brand-name tablets when they were supplied in branded packets to those who normally used those anyway. If they didn't have their name on the packet, they weren't so effective, even amongst women who normally used them. Women who usually used other brands got more relief from the brand-name pills when they didn't know what they were – i.e. if they were given no-name packets. The placebos brought a fair amount of relief, both when provided in branded and unbranded packets, but less than either the branded or unbranded analgesic.

The researchers concluded that headache relief was therefore not all in the mind but could be aided by belief in the powers of a product, either because that product had been tried before or because someone else made claims for it.

Some advertisers use the 'home trial' to capitalise on the psychological effects of commitment. The action of cutting out a coupon, filling it in and remembering to post it may predispose one to feel favourably towards a product in order to justify one's investment of energy so far. Similarly, encouraging shoppers to participate in product trials in supermarkets may work to make them feel favourably disposed towards the product in question. As we saw in Chapter 6, role playing of any kind strengthens identification with the role, even if it is one to which the actor is normally opposed.

In the 1950s there was an outcry over subliminal advertising, when it was discovered that messages or pictures one couldn't quite see were being slipped into advertisements, posters and films. The messages were designed to predispose the viewer to buy a certain product without realising that his urge to do so was anything other than self-willed. Although it remained highly dubious whether such techniques were effective, the practice was banned in Britain and some American states.

Much quoted, to fan the fear of such insidious attack on autonomy, has been Norman Dixon's finding, in 1955, that when he presented to subjects words that were just below the threshold at which they are registered consciously and then asked them to say the first word that came into their heads, they chose words that had some meaningful connection with the word they had just seen subliminally.

R. Jung showed that, in sleep, the mind responded (measurably, by special instruments) to 'faint but significant sounds' such as the whispering of an individual's name. The individual would not wake or, if he did, he wouldn't have registered why. This showed that some part of the brain was able to respond to low-key stimuli, presumably in case the stimuli signified a potential threat, whilst the person remained unaware that anything had occurred and been registered.

Whilst such findings proved that subliminal advertising might be effective, and therefore was unethical, more recent findings of a similar ilk have allowed advertisers to capitalise on the fruits of research without resorting to anything overtly controversial. Discoveries about the differing roles of the left and right hemispheres of the brain have shown that the left-brain is the conscious, logical side while the right-brain is more concerned with intuitive, creative thought. The left-brain, being dominant in Western society (emphasis being placed on intellectual skills), tends to drown out the right-brain, which only achieves dominance when the other is 'switched off', as during sleep or relaxation or meditation. Advertisers don't mind if television viewers watching a film mentally 'switch off' when the adverts come on, and talk to each other or pick up a newspaper. The right brain is still watching.

It is perhaps interesting that subliminal advertising created the uproar that it did. It was patently not fair play. And yet, in advertising generally, it is not the overt message that is important, it is the hidden message, that stirs up largely unconscious guilt or insecurity which can be relieved by purchasing the product.

Institutions

A total institution was defined by Erving Goffman in *Asylums* as 'a place of residence and work where a large number of like-situated individuals, cut off from the wider society for an appreciable period of time, together lead an enclosed, formally administered round of life'. Because inmates of such institutions – such as nunneries, prisons, mental hospitals – have limited contact with the world outside, and therefore no reference points outside of the institution, their supervisors can control not only their actions but the stimuli they receive and the way they respond to their environment. The institution can shape behaviour by rewarding approved traits and discouraging others.

Brown asks, in *Techniques of Persuasion*, 'whether the Communists have devised any method which is half as efficient in "brainwashing" (or with results that are half as permanent) as the English public school'. Public schools, whose pupils are traditionally drawn from the sons of the moneyed classes, do much to further the socialisation effects that Toch has described, whereby early experience and indoctrination is reinforced when an individual proceeds to mingle with others who have shared a similar upbringing.

Corrective institutions, however, can go further, in the name of therapy. An American programme designed to reform juvenile delinquents was described by Packard in *The People Shapers*. Youths who embarked on what was called the Seed programme were isolated from their friends and families and lived as a group where they were stripped of their old identities and given a lowly position in a very organised hierarchical structure. The 'seedling' could only advance up the hierarchy by learning to 'think right', in the reformers' terms. Older seedlings on the programme subjected the new seedling to intense peer pressure to conform and watched him to make sure he didn't backslide. (Seedlings who could inform on a renegade were suitably rewarded.) One seedling was quoted as saying that an older seedling even came with him whenever he went to the bathroom.

The programme was so criticised because of its effects that it became the subject of a US Senate hearing. One school counsellor testified that when the seedlings returned to their old schools they were certainly reformed but they also seemed to be like zombies and refused to associate with any children who had not been seedlings. She said: 'Seedlings seem to have an informing system on each other and on others that is similar to Nazi Germany. They run in to use

the telephone daily to report against each other to the Seed.'
The programme was discontinued.

In 1961 the American Federal Bureau of Prisons held a
conference for associate wardens to which speakers on
behaviour change and reform were invited. One was Edgar
Schein who spoke on the thought reform techniques used in
Korea.

Schein said that he thought the tactics themselves were
legitimate, it was the ends that were suspect in the Chinese
case. (Later he changed his stand and said that, were he to give
his talk again, he would advise against the use of such tactics in
prison as a means of reform.) Whether the information he
provided in his talk had any bearing or not, a programme very
similar to thought reform was instituted in Marion Peniten-
tiary in Illinois. A petition submitted in complaint to the
United Nations Economic and Social Council in 1972 listed
all the similiarities, such as segregation of prison leaders, the
encouraging of prisoner spying on prisoner, tricked statements, undermining of emotional supports, placing prisoners
in ambiguous situations to create confusion, the use of
humiliations and insults, the rewarding of submission and the
fostering of the illusion amongst isolated prisoners that each
had been abandoned by his social peer group.

Both programmes were carried out in the name of therapy
and in the belief that the values and standards being imposed
on the 'victims' were those that right-minded individuals
should hold.

Sometimes the ambience of an institution can influence
behaviour in unsuspected and unintended ways. John
McVicar, in his autobiography written while on the run from
prison, claimed that the prison system could not hope to be
reformative because, in effect, it served to romanticise the
hardened con. Young prisoners were more likely to identify
with the tough long-termers than with the prison wardens; so
the spurious image of the glamorous macho life of the
hardened criminal was perpetuated rather than dissipated.

Life in prisons and on long-stay wards in mental hospitals
can lead to institutionalisation, as it is now called. Years on

end spent in the same environment without any real stimulation can reduce a person to a vegetable. This is exactly what was recognised to have happened to mental patients in the fifties, a discovery which led to a new approach to psychiatric care. Patients used to sit all day on drab wards with nothing to do. They had no need to take any responsibility for themselves, as all meals were provided, beds made and no living had to be earned. The patients became utterly dependent and incapable of initiating any action for themselves. In mental hospitals today, patients are encouraged to take responsibility for themselves and to participate in occupational therapy of various kinds but in some hospitals, particularly mental handicap hospitals, overcrowding and poor staff levels still work to deny patients the attention they need as human beings. Often the result is the development of disruptive behaviour patterns, purely as an attention-getting means.

As Hinkle pointed out, in the context of prisoners under interrogation, lack of stimulation endured during confinement can adversely affect the brain and speed its deterioration. We are shocked to read, for instance, of a brilliant scientist who for a long time has been held the captive of a hostile government and returns to the world a broken man, incapable of carrying on his work. Yet, in old people's homes everywhere, people are being precipitated into senility because they too are starved of the stimulus of a changing environment. They may look at bright curtains instead of cell walls every day but the effects are largely the same. In such ways, institutions can manipulate as a result of well-intentioned ignorance rather than malicious design.

Institutions and organisations of all kinds, by their very nature, need to establish rules, hierarchies and permitted modes of behaviour in order to fit all their members into their framework. Whereas an institution may be created, initially, to meet the needs of a certain group, eventually the needs of the institution itself overtake those it was designed to meet. Thus trades unions become vast unwieldy beasts, with decisions taken at regional and national levels, far removed from their members. The 1981 election for a deputy leader of the Labour Party in Britain revealed that the larger trades unions were so out of touch with their shop floor members that they lacked even the machinery to consult them.

Institutions teach conformity and obedience to authority, using ascent up the hierarchy as the accepted and conventional reward. Innovations within firms such as worker-directors or power-sharing are doomed to failure if old conditioning is not replaced by new training. Ensuing chaos is seen as proof that a new system can't work instead of being seen as evidence that social attitudes need to be changed *before* a system is altered.

Institutions that one elects to join, such as church organisations or commercial corporations, may instil more conformity to societal norms than any corrective institution can achieve. For the individual effectually exercises the choice to join and therefore the choice to conform. The amorphous, ubiquitous 'they' who control things were once the boys at the bottom.

10 RESISTING INFLUENCE

Is it possible to resist strong influence of an overt or subtle kind? Sargant maintains that any normal person will eventually crack under interrogation, if the pressure is kept up long enough. Yet there are known occasions of successful resistance against brainwashing techniques. In Korea, for instance, while a third of the American POWs capitulated in some way to their captors, the Turks who suffered the same treatments in the same camps did not collaborate in even the most minor ways. Nor did any of their men die in captivity, whereas hundreds of Americans did.

Whereas the American morale was low, the Turks deliberately kept morale high. If one of their number became ill, others were assigned to feed and bathe him, to ensure that he had a chance to recover. Internal discipline was maintained at all costs. Whereas the Americans suffered psychologically from the Chinese tactic of removing leaders from the rest of the group, the Turks implemented a solution which prevented the Chinese from breaking down their morale. If the Turkish officer in command was removed, his role was assumed by the next man down. If that man was removed, the command shifted downwards again and so it would go on until, if necessary, a private was in command.

The Turkish response to the Chinese interrogation techniques was derision. Their mass resistance won the day.

Brown, in his analysis of the events in Korea in *Techniques of Persuasion*, came to the conclusion that lack of morale among the prisoners who collaborated was the main factor in leaving them vulnerable to Chinese coercion techniques. He pointed out that 'in any form of persuasion, from the mildest to the most severe, it is always the case that those who refuse to cooperate are in no danger while those who give the slightest indication of doing so are doomed'.

The validity of that comment might well be attested to by any who have expressed mild interest in the wares of a door-to-door salesman, either out of politeness or mild curiosity. Jessica Mitford, in *Hons and Rebels*, describes the 'brain-washing' effects of the salesman's technique if he is just allowed that opening in order to pitch in:

> 'In essence it consisted of a deft combination of mental torture and physical manipulation designed to reduce the subject to a state of helpless passivity, bereft of independent will and ready to sign anything as a condition of freedom from torment.'

Many investigators of the Korean experience have noted tactics which seemed to help resisters resist. It is of interest that most are common-sense notions that emphasise the need to develop and maintain a correct perspective on life – ordinary life.

Much mentioned as a means of getting information and situations into correct perspective is humour. Meerloo points out that the demagogue is almost incapable of humour of any kind. Fervour effectively leaves no room for laughter. But if the demagogue is *treated* with humour, he is out of his element and starts to collapse.

The ability to laugh means the ability to see how things should be. Jokes work by highlighting ridiculous behaviour or by providing an unexpected perspective on a given situation. (Lady Astor to Winston Churchill at a dinner party: 'Mr Churchill, if I were married to you, I should put poison in your coffee.' Mr Churchill: 'Madam, if I were married to you, I should drink the coffee.'). The graffiti that appears on public walls, of sufficient wit to find its way into published collections of the stuff, is all about alternative ways of arranging available information.

The momentary suspension of belief that operates when a joke is being heard allows the hearer to open his mind to new ways of seeing a perhaps familiar scenario or a new way of interpreting familiar behaviour patterns. A joke is funny because it confounds one's normal expectations of how things turn out and when we hear a joke, we invite our expectations to be confounded. 'Serious' information is less easily assimilated if it goes against our established beliefs.

Because the ability to laugh signifies the ability to suspend belief and to see or hear what *is* instead of what we expect to see or hear, it enables us to recognise distortion when it confronts us, according to Meerloo. How can the demagogue be taken seriously? But to be effective, the demagogue must be taken seriously.

Sargant makes the point that the best way to avoid conversion of any kind is not to get emotionally involved in the proceedings. Once guilt, fear, anger are stirred up, one is half way to being won. Therefore, he concludes:

'The obstacles that the religious or political proselytizer cannot overcome are indifference or detached, controlled and continued amusement on the part of the subject at the efforts being made to break him down or win him over or tempt him into argument. The safety of the free world seems therefore to lie in a cultivation not only of courage, moral virtue and logic but of humour: humour which produces the well-balanced state in which emotional excess is laughed at as ugly and wasteful.'

The Turks made use of humour when they derided the propaganda of the Chinese. Investigation of the crew of the US spy ship, *Pueblo*, which was captured off the Korean coast in 1968, showed that those who stood out most easily against 'confessing' to criminal acts were those who used humour, among other things, as a defence mechanism.

Humour is therefore not only a tool for keeping one's own perspective balanced but an aid, via its absence, to identifying those others who have no sense of perspective. Beware the leaders of causes, salesmen and experts who cannot genuinely laugh at themselves.

The need to detach oneself emotionally from a pressured situation was also identified in an experiment by Zimbardo.

As part of his work for the US Office of Naval Research, Zimbardo carried out his now famous prison experiment. He advertised in the papers for healthy male volunteers and, of the 75 applicants, the 24 most emotionally stable were selected. None had prison records. On an arbitrary basis, half were assigned to be prison guards, the rest to be prisoners. The 'prison' was a mock-up built in the basement at Stanford university. The guards were told they had to keep order but that they couldn't resort to physical punishments of any kind.

Zimbardo actually arranged for the prisoners to be 'arrested' on the day set for the experiment to begin. Police cars collected them from their homes, they were handcuffed, then photographed and finger-printed at the police station before being taken to the prison, where their clothes were replaced by prison garb (a smock, no underwear, prison number on the back of the smock, and a nylon cap which covered the hair and therefore made the men look pretty much the same). The guards wore khaki uniforms.

The prisoners then started a normal type prison routine – work, limited visiting rights, bland food at mealtimes – and by the second day, signs of extreme stress were already evident, including depression and crying and very acute anxiety. The guards, meanwhile, were enjoying their new power and were upset when the experiment was called to a halt earlier than intended because of the effects it was having on the prisoners. (Later the guards professed themselves amazed at the degree to which they had indulged their power, harassing and provoking the prisoners.)

That the experience had been 'real' to the prisoners was shown by incidents such as the following. Several came before a 'parole' board asking to be allowed to be released, for which they would give up their pay for taking part in the experiment. The parole officer (Zimbardo) said he would think about it and the prisoners went quietly back to their cells, although any of them could just have insisted on being released there and then.

While the experiment was going on, Zimbardo monitored the private conversations of the prisoners. He found that 90 per cent of it was concerned with the prison conditions and how bad everything was there. They allowed the misery induced by being in the prison to dominate their lives and conversations, thus increasing the intensity of its effects. They did not escape from it mentally by talking with each other about their real lives outside or about any other topics of general interest.

The experiment is commonly cited to show the power of the prison environment to influence the behaviour of those in power and those under it. But Peter Watson, in *War on the Mind*, suggests that the real purpose of the experiment was to find out how prisoners of war can be taught to withstand the pressures of their captivity. Firstly, it was the US Navy that financed the study. Secondly the simulated prisoners were men with clean records. They had not taken a risk by committing a crime, and failed, thus incurring punishment. They were men who could feel their incarceration was unjust, which was more the case for captured servicemen than convicted prisoners. Thirdly, their heads were all covered by nylon caps – a symbolic shaving of the head which occurred in prison camps but not in prisons – and the guards wore khaki – military rather than civilian style?

What the experiment therefore revealed was that, in prisoner of war camps, the very worst thing was for prisoners to wallow in their condition and allow it to overcome them. They should avoid harping on the vicissitudes of their environment and make efforts to escape mentally by turning their attention to other things. If they did bow to their sufferings, they ended up not only denigrating themselves but denigrating each other (as the experimental prisoners did) which further served to weaken group ties.

In *Among the Dervishes*, O. M. Burke describes a conversation with a Turkish Sufi who claimed that the only way he and his co-fighters survived in Korea was by the practice of getting together every day and telling stories about the perfectibility of mankind, the destiny of the human race and qualities such as generosity and love.

Getting outside a situation is one of the best ways of seeing it for what it is instead of becoming swamped by it and helpless to resist. People who suffer from depression are commonly advised not to keep thinking about the bad times, or to read distressing news reports or to keep going back to places that recall the memory of someone lost, because each serves to reinforce the feeling of depression. 'Snapping out of it', however, becomes impossible if the depression *is* allowed to take hold. Immersion in any experience mars one's judgement about its import and its true relationship to other events in life.

Jacobo Timerman, who underwent imprisonment and torture in Argentina, described how he detached himself emotionally from his predicament, in order to save himself from succumbing to it:

'I realised that, instinctively, I'd developed an attitude of absolute passivity. This passivity, I believe, preserved a great deal of energy. . . . I felt I was becoming a vegetable, casting aside all logical emotions and sensations – fear, hatred, vengeance – for any emotion or sensation meant wasting useless energy.

'. . . Both parties seem to feel some need of the other: for the torturer, it is a sense of omnipotence, without which he'd find it hard perhaps to exercise his profession – the torturer needs to be needed by the tortured; whereas the man who's tortured finds in his torturer a human voice, a dialogue for his situation, some partial exercise of his human condition – he asks for pity, to go to the bathroom, for another plate of soup. He asks for the result of a football game.

'I was able to avoid all that.' (*Observer*, July 19, 1981.)

By emotional detachment of whatever means, political prisoners have thus been able to preserve their integrity. Their situation, by the very fact it is extreme, serves to highlight the fact that emotional involvement in any cir-

cumstance can affect one's judgement of it. The kindly con-
man regularly takes advantage of that one.

Emotions colour perceptions. Once that is recognised one
can say, 'Just because I like him/he excites me/he sympa-
thises with me, it doesn't mean he knows how to invest my
money.'

The opposite of emotional detachment is emotional self-
centredness, to which insecure people all too often fall prey.
Thus if, in conversation, the insecure person hears someone
say, 'I find it difficult to relate to people who are self-
opinionated,' he will start to worry, 'I wonder if he thinks *I'm*
self-opinionated,' and start to act defensively. The speaker
may not have considered the matter at all, it may even be
irrelevant to the particular conversation, but the listener, by
relating all he hears back to himself, opts to place himself in a
vulnerable position. He is always too anxious about what
people might think about *him* to hear anything they have to
say about anything else.

Several commentators on Korea have pointed out that
soldiers who were uncertain of their facts or who accepted
ideas blindly were the more susceptible to influence. One is
the more susceptible to persuasive reasoning if one has never
cultivated the capacity to think for oneself, to ask questions,
to check facts, or, in other words, to take responsibility for
the information one accepts. The result is often an inability
to distinguish between fact and opinion.

The main thrust of health education today is to encourage
people to take more responsibility for their own health
instead of leaving it to their doctors. The *Good Health
Guide*, a general readership publication produced by The
Open University in association with the Health Education
Council and the Scottish Health Education Unit, emphasises the individual's responsibility to question assumptions
about health:

'We are all selective about the information we retain and
what we believe. One of the key factors affecting this is our
own position in life. For example, if you smoke 50

cigarettes a day and can't give them up you will resist accepting the fact that cigarettes cause lung cancer. Someone who has never smoked and finds cigarettes unpleasant will find this fact easy to believe. (It *is* a fact, scientifically proved. What is still a matter of opinion is how cigarettes cause lung cancer.)

'Similarly, if you are well off, you may find it hard to accept the fact that poor people have much more illness than people who are comfortably off. It may make you feel guilty. However, if you are poor, you know it's true – ill-health is part of your life. The relationship between money and ill-health is a fact. What is still open to opinion is *why* poor people are less healthy.

'Some opinions are eventually shown to be facts, others aren't. So you need to think carefully about your "facts" and try to check whether they are really opinions. Try asking yourself these two questions: Where did I get the information from? What personal interest do I have in believing or not believing certain information?'

An unwitting emotional investment in believing certain 'facts' may impair one's intellectual detachment. Unquestioning acceptance of partial truths may also lead to erroneous beliefs. We are led to believe, by advertisers, that certain sweets and chocolates give us energy. That is quite true. What they omit to say is that all foods provide energy. If, by that omission, the public comes to believe that, if you want to up your energy levels, you should eat sweets and chocolates, the advertisers have achieved their aim and the public has been duped.

Investigating why one holds a belief protects one from being influenced as a result of ignorance. The belief in fact ceases to be belief. It is replaced by knowledge.

Belief-testing is one means of taking responsibility for oneself instead of passing it to others, a tendency that was highlighted in a previous chapter. Just as relinquishing responsibility was mentioned as one reason for becoming susceptible to influence, so exercising subjective control, in however limited circumstances, can have the converse effect, according to Biderman. He has described the tactic of a man who was tortured during interrogation by the Gestapo and who knew that the point would come where he could not prevent himself from passing out. However, he found that he could 'control' the point at which he fainted by deciding 'I will not pass out for another sixty seconds'. This minor evidence that he could still in some way control what happened to him enabled him to maintain his mastery of the situation and he didn't crack during several months of intense interrogation. He remained, in his own mind, acting rather than acted upon.

Even Timerman's passivity, during his torture in Argentina, was a consciously adopted stance, chosen as a means of retaining as much control over himself, his actions and his responses as he could under the circumstances.

An everyday example of a minor exercise of control affecting one's perceptions of self and situation is the feminist tactic (recommended by American therapist and feminist Betty Dodson) for not being treated as a sex object. Many women dislike receiving admiring catcalls, suggestive offers, or explicit comments on their anatomy from men they pass in the street. They feel embarrassed and helpless to express the hostility they feel. Every such experience just reinforces their feeling that they are seen simply as sex objects and that they have no control over the situation. The feminist response is to act on the situation to change its nature.

> 'When men make approaches in the street [says Betty], I give them the kind of eye contact I'd give an old friend. I smile, say, "Hi, lovely day", treat him as a mate I've known for years. And make really polite conversation. The fact that he is actually contacting *with* me rather than *at* me alters his whole attitude. He begins to see me as a person, rather than a sex object. And he stops bothering me.' (*Psychology Today*, UK, Jan. 1979, p. 25.)

By such a trivial ploy a woman can effectually reinforce for herself the conviction that she can influence, instead of just be influenced by, such encounters. Learned helplessness, as was shown in Chapter 4, is purely a product of faulty conditioning and, once one is aware of it, can be reversed.

The fixed idea is the enemy of all free thinking. It is far more difficult to accept that two opposing ideas may not be mutually exclusive than, in a desire for absolutes, to plump for one or the other. That two opposing *actions* may not be mutually exclusive either was neatly demonstrated by American psychologist Ulrich Neisser and colleagues. They demonstrated that it is possible for people to learn to read and write simultaneously without losing concentration. Their subjects were required to read short stories and, at the same time, take down dictation about something else. At first they found the task impossible but, after six weeks, their reading speeds were normal and their dictation correct. To check that the subjects had not resorted to 'automatic pilot' for one of the activities, while concentrating on the other, the researchers tested them for understanding of both what they had read and what they had written. The subjects had absorbed all the material. They could literally be more 'open minded' than they had imagined possible.

All the studies of the American prisoners of war in Korea showed that those who had stable, integrated personalities were the least likely to succumb to Communist propaganda. The important thing was to have a balanced perspective on life.

Most therapists emphasise that the key to mental health is to accept life for what it is, and face it for what it is, instead of working on the basis of what we want it to be. To accept life for what it is, we first have to know how it is and that must include an understanding of how conditioning and emotions and needs and assumptions can affect our behaviour and our perceptions. Only if we know that sometimes we act a certain way because we are looking for social approval and another time we react a certain way because we want attention or security, can we make realistic judgements about causes and effects.

Philip Zimbardo is currently working on a research project to test the hypothesis that a tendency to overlook realistic causes for inexplicable occurrences may actually be a cause of certain mental illnesses. He hypnotised a group of students to suffer an impairment to their hearing when he said a certain word. The word was spoken later during a discussion session with other students. Afterwards he found out that the students who had been hypnotised were convinced that other people were talking about them and wanting to harm them, because it was assumed that everyone else must be whispering. Zimbardo suggests that many paranoid elderly people may become so because they don't realise they are losing their hearing. They accuse family and friends of whispering about them and the family and friends, so amazed by the bizarre behaviour, then do start to worry and talk about them behind their backs.

Similarly, he says, a person may develop a phobia of lifts because one day when he is feeling queasy he happens to get into a lift. He then decides the lift must be making him feel sick.

Many emotional problems, according to Zimbardo, could be caused by inappropriate blame.

We can't be impervious to external influences. Even the weather, it is now known, can affect us physiologically and emotionally, although, in our ignorance, we may assume that our debility or depression is due to some other cause. Perhaps it is only by standing back, emotionally, and testing our assumptions that we can become more the masters of ourselves and correspondingly less the slaves of circumstance.

BIBLIOGRAPHY AND ACKNOWLEDGEMENTS

The author wishes gratefully to acknowledge all the books and articles referred to in the text. These are listed below and are all highly recommended reading.

Abelson, R. P., E. Aronson, W. J. McGuire, T. M. Newcomb, M. J. Rosenberg & P. H. Tannenbaum, *Theories of Cognitive Consistency: a sourcebook,* Rand McNally & Co., Chicago, 1968.

Aronson, E., *The Social Animal*, W. H. Freeman, San Francisco, 1976.

Aronson, E. & D. Linder, 'Gain and loss of esteem as determinants of interpersonal attractiveness', *Journal of Experimental Social Psychology*, 1, 176–81.

Askenasy, Hans, *Are we all Nazis?*, Lyle Stuart, New Jersey, 1978.

Barber, Joe, Research reported at the Psychology and Medicine Conference in Swansea, held by the Welsh Branch of the British Psychological Society, 1979.

Biderman, Albert O. & Herbert Zimmer, *The Manipulation of Human Behaviour*, John Wiley, New York, 1961.

Bowart, Walter, *Operation Mind Control*, Fontana, London, 1978.

Brehm, S. W. and A. R. Cohen, *Explorations in Cognitive Dissonance*, Wiley, New York, 1962.

Brown, J. A. C., *Techniques of Persuasion*, Pelican, London, 1963.

Bugliosi, V. and C. Gentry, *Helter Skelter*, The Bodley Head, London, 1975.

Canetti, Elias, *Crowds and Power*, Victor Gollancz, London, 1962.

214   *The Manipulated Mind*

Conway, Flo and Jim Siegelman, *Snapping*, Delta Books, New York, 1978.

Crutchfield, R. S., 'Conformity and character', in Wrightman, *Contemporary Issues in Social Psychology*, California, Brooks/Cole, 1968.

Dicks, Henry V., *Licensed Mass Murder*, Sussex University Press/Heinemann, London, 1972.

Ellson, D. G., 'Hallucinations produced by sensory conditioning', *Journal of Experimental Psychology*, 1941, **28**, 1–20.

Erikson, E., *Childhood and Society*, Norton, New York, 1950.

Eysenck, Hans & Michael Eysenck, *Mindwatching*, Michael Joseph, London, 1981.

Field, Peter B. & Samuel F. Dworkin, 'Strategies of hypnotic investigation', *Journal of Psychology*, 1967, **67**, 47–58.

Frank, Jerome D., *Persuasion and Healing*, The Johns Hopkins Press, 1961/Schocken Books, NY, 1963, 1970.

Frankel, H. & M. T. Orne, 'Hypnotizability and phobic behaviour', *Archives of General Psychiatry*, Vol. 33, 1976, 1259–61.

Freedman, J. L. & S. C. Fraser, 'Compliance without pressure: the foot in the door technique', *Journal of Personality & Social Psychology*, 1966, **4**, 197–201.

Goodall, Kenneth, 'Shapers at work', *Psychology Today*, Nov. 1972, 132–3.

Greenspoon, J. 'The reinforcing effect of two spoken sounds on the frequency of two responses', *American Journal of Psychology*, 1955, **68**, 409–416.

Hinkle Jr., Lawrence E. & Harold G. Wolff, 'The methods of interrogation and indoctrination used by the Communist State Police', *Bulletin of the NY Academy of Medicine*, Sept. 1957.

Hinkle Jr, Lawrence E., 'The physiological state of the interrogation subject as it affects brain function', *Manipulation of Human Behaviour* (see Biderman).

Hoffer, Eric, *The True Believer*, Secker & Warburg, London, 1952.

Hoffman, M. L., 'Conformity as a defence mechanism and a form of resistance to genuine group influence', *Journal of Personality*, 1957, **25**, 412–24.

Hyde, Margaret O., *Brainwashing and Other Forms of Mind Control*, McGraw-Hill, New York, 1977.

Kennedy, Ludovic, *Ten Rillington Place*, Victor Gollancz, London, 1961.

Kiesler, Charles A., *The Psychology of Commitment*, Academic Press, New York, 1971.

Kiesler, C. A. & S. B. Kiesler, 'Role of forewarning in persuasive communications', *Journal of Abnormal & Social Psychology*, 1964, **68**, 547–9.

Koestler, Arthur, *The God that Failed*, Bantam, NY, 1952.

Krasner, Leonard, 'Behaviour control and social responsibility', *American Psychologist*, 1964, **17**, 199–204.

Latané, B. & J. M. Darley, *The Unresponsive Bystander: why doesn't he help?*, Appleton-Century-Crofts, New York, 1970.

Lifton, Robert Jay, *Thought Reform and the Psychology of Totalism*, Victor Gollancz, London, 1961.

London, Perry, *Behaviour Control*, Harper & Row, New York, 1969.

Loomis, A. L., E. N. Harvey & G. Hobart, 'Brain potentials during hypnosis', *Science*, 1936, 239–41.

Jung, R., *Brain Mechanism and Consciousness*, Blackwell, Oxford, 1954.

Marks, John, *The Search for the 'Manchurian Candidate'*, Time Books/Allen Lane, New York, 1979.

McCarthy, M., 'The hue and cry' in *The Writing on the Wall*, Penguin, Harmondsworth, 1969.

McGuire, W. J. & S. Millman, 'Anticipating belief lowering following forewarning of a persuasive attack', *Journal of Personality & Social Psychology*, 1965, **2**, 471–9.

McKenzie, Ian K., 'Hostage-captor relationships', *Bulletin of the British Psychological Society*, 1981, **34**, 161–3.

Meerloo, Joost, A. M., *Mental Seduction and Menticide: the psychology of thought control and brainwashing*, Jonathan Cape, London, 1957.

Milgram, Stanley, *Obedience to Authority*, Harper & Row, New York, 1974.

Mitford, Jessica, *Kind and Usual Punishment*, Alfred A. Knopf, New York, 1973.

Murray, E. J., 'A content analysis method of studying psychotherapy', *Psychological Monographs*, **70**, 420.

Orne, M. T., 'The nature of hypnosis, artifact and essence', *Journal of Abnormal & Social Psychology*, 1959, **58**, 277–9.

Orne, M. T., 'The potential uses of hypnosis in interrogation' in *The Manipulation of Human Behaviour* (see Biderman).

Packard, Vance, *The People Shapers*, Little, Brown & Co., Boston, 1977.

Pear, T. H., *The Moulding of Man*, George Allen & Unwin, London, 1961.

Qualter, T. H., *Propaganda and Psychological Warfare*, Random House, New York, 1962.

Ramage, Ian, *Battle for the Free Mind*, George Allen & Unwin, London, 1967.

Rogers, Carl R. & B. F. Skinner, 'Some issues concerning the control of human behaviour', *Science*, **124**, 1057–66, Nov. 30 1956.

Rosenthal, D., 'Changes in some moral values following psychotherapy', *Journal of Consulting Psychology*, 1955, **19**, 431–436.

Salter, Andrew, *Conditioned Reflex Therapy,* NY Capricorn Books, 1949/1961.

Sarbin, T. R., & D. T. Lim, 'Some evidence in support of role-taking hypothesis in hypnosis', *International Journal of Clinical Hypnosis*, 1936, **11**, 98–103.

Sargant, William, *Battle for the Mind*, Heinemann, London, 1957.

Schatzman, M., *The Story of Ruth*, Duckworth, London, 1980.

Scheflin, Alan W. & Edward M. Opton Jr., *The Mind Manipulators*, Paddington Press, London, 1978.

Schein, Edgar, 'Distinguishing characteristics of

collaborators and resisters among American prisoners of war', *Journal of Abnormal Psychology*, 1950, **55**, 197–201.

Schein, Edgar, 'The Chinese indoctrination programme for prisoners of war', *Psychiatry*, 1956, **19**, 149–72.

Schils, E., 'Authoritarianism right and left', in *Studies in the Scope and Method of Authoritarian Personality* (eds Christie & Jajoda), The Free Press, Glencoe, Illinois, 1954.

Seligman, M., 'Falling into helplessness', *Psychology Today*, UK, Vol. 1, issue 1, 46.

Skinner, B. F., see Rogers.

Toch, Hans, *The Social Psychology of Social Movements*, Methuen, London, 1966.

Vernon, Jack, *Inside the Black Room: studies of sensory deprivation*, Pelican, Harmondsworth, 1963.

Watson, Peter, *War on the Mind*, Hutchinson, London, 1978.

Whorf, Benjamin Lee, 'The relation of habitual thought and behaviour to language', in *Language, Culture & Personality*, Sapir Memorial Publication Fund, 1941.

Zimbardo, Philip, Ebbe Ebbeson & Christina Maslach, *Influencing Attitudes and Changing Behaviour*, Addison Wesley, Reading, Mass., 1969/1977.

Other Malor Books

BATTLE FOR THE MIND
by William Sargant

How can an evangelist convert a hardboiled sophisticate? Why does a POW sign a "confession" that he knows is false? How is a criminal pressured into admitting his guilt? Do the evangelist, the POW's captor, and the policeman use similar methods to gain their ends?

These and other compelling questions are discussed in the definitive work by William Sargant, who for many years until his death in 1988 was a leading physician in psychological medicine. Sargant spells out and illustrates the basic technique used by evangelists, psychiatrists and brain-washers to disperse the patterns of belief and behavior already established in the minds of their hearers, and to substitute new patterns for them.

From the Preface:
"This mechanism holds the possibility of explaining and understanding much of how people suddenly change direction in life, and some of the strangest religious and spiritual behavior ever described among human beings... Perhaps most important, understanding it can give us insight into the formation of social bonds, the development of gangs and groups, and allow us to make more informed choices as individuals, as a society and as a culture, how we want our own groups to develop."
Charles Swencionis, Ph.D.
Albert Einstein College of Medicine

A MALOR BOOK

ISBN: 1-883536-06-5 • *Paper* • *332 pages (including 23 black and white plates)*

THE MIND FIELD
by Robert Ornstein, Ph.D.

For years, Westerners have been seeking rational, analytical answers to despair and anxiety. But now, this rational Western perception of consciousness has been challenged by an Eastern discipline which brings into sharp focus the travesty and deception underlying many of the contemporary awareness movements.

However, the excesses of the self-improvement packagers obscure what may be of real value. Meditation may be a valid method for eliminating stress, but are maharishis and franchised growth centers the requisites for achieving peace of mind? How is it that promoters have supplanted real teachers in the realm of consciousness? Ornstein extends his argument to the sacrosanct psychiatric profession, as well as to meditation, parapsychologies, shamanism, and the numerous trademarked "awareness systems."

Yet, it is also Ornstein's intent to combat the easy criticisms of the super-rationalists who dismiss every new development as the irresponsible invention of the "guru-of-the-month club." He offers not only the findings of extensive scientific research on the brain but the valuable discoveries of personal experience as well. There is no one who is better qualified to assess our modern approach to matters of the mind than Robert Ornstein, and he does so with clarity, wit, and utter persuasiveness.

"Works with cool logic and scientific skepticism to point up the potential of intuitional, inductive, and holistic modes of thought, while separating out the voguish chaff."

—The New York Times

A MALOR BOOK

ISBN: 1-883536-00-6 • *Paper* • *144 pages*

Zimbardo
    Influencing Attitudes &
       Changing Behavior